'Through the eyes, ears, nose and mind of one autistic woman, *Sensing the City* takes us on a vividly described and detailed journey through urban landscapes. Sandra highlights many of the tiny elements that make autistic life both stressful and magical on a moment by moment basis.'

— *Sarah Hendrickx, autistic adult and Autism Consultant*

'This book makes it clear just how important sensory sensitivities can be to an autistic individual. Whilst these are usually seen in a negative light, the author stresses the positive aspects as well, and in doing so, follows in the footsteps of Temple Grandin and others.'

— *Nick Chown, author of* Understanding and Evaluating Autism Theory

SENSING THE CITY

AN AUTISTIC PERSPECTIVE

SANDRA BEALE-ELLIS
FOREWORD BY LUKE BEARDON

Jessica Kingsley *Publishers*
London and Philadelphia

First published in 2017
by Jessica Kingsley Publishers
73 Collier Street
London N1 9BE, UK
and
400 Market Street, Suite 400
Philadelphia, PA 19106, USA

www.jkp.com

Library of Congress Cataloging in Publication Data
Title: Sensing the city : an autistic perspective / Sandra Beale-Ellis.
Description: London ; Philadelphia : Jessica Kingsley Publishers, 2017. |
    Includes bibliographical references and index.
Identifiers: LCCN 2017029088 (print) | LCCN 2017013155 (ebook) |
ISBN
    9781784501150 (ebook) | ISBN 9781849056359 (alk. paper)
Subjects: LCSH: Autistic people. | Senses and sensation. | City and town
life.
Classification: LCC RC553.A88 (print) | LCC RC553.A88 B43 2017
(ebook) | DDC
    616.85/882--dc23

British Library Cataloguing in Publication Data
A CIP catalogue record for this book is available from the British Library

ISBN 978 1 84905 635 9
eISBN 978 1 78450 115 0

Printed and bound in the United States

For Joe who lived this book with me, my parents who raised me, and my fur babies who always comfort me. I love you all.

ACKNOWLEDGEMENTS

Thanks to all the named and unnamed autistic individuals who have provided examples and inspiration for *Sensing the City*.

Thanks to my parents-in-law for always supporting me; Ricky, I miss you and wish you could have read this book.

Thanks to my friends and family members who calmed me when I was feeling overwhelmed and tired during the research and writing of this book.

A special thanks to my friend, colleague and critical eye, Dr Luke Beardon, for writing the foreword to *Sensing the City*, and providing me with constant encouragement and detailed feedback on so many projects; because of you, I am a better writer.

Lastly, it is a pleasure to personally thank Jessica Kingsley, my editor and publisher, and her team. Without your continued support, this book may never have completed its journey. Thank you for believing in me.

CONTENTS

ENTERTAINMENT

FOREWORD

I've known Sandra for many years now, and it is no surprise to me whatsoever that she has produced such a fascinating read for publication. The journey she's been on (figuratively, as well as literally) to getting this done has not always been easy. There have been times when Sandra shared with me that it was all too much, and she was considering not completing it. Privately, I gave myself a wry smile and thought, 'Yeah, whatever, Sandra…I'll believe that when I see it' – because she simply never gives up, on anything as far as I can tell. However challenging, daunting or problematic a situation she finds herself in, she fights on with what can only be described as inspirational spirit. And she tends to end up winning! I have had the immense privilege to have known Sandra in a plethora of different guises, and in each one she has shown the same determination to give it her best – and Sandra's best is usually pretty good in my experience.

Decades ago I met a young autistic man who shared with me that the reason he always tried to run away when it was time for his evening shower as a (non-verbal) child was because each droplet of water felt like a pin prick on his skin, such that the experience of standing under a shower was akin to torture. When I discussed this with his parents they were – understandably – horrified. They wanted to know how this could have been the case: Why hadn't they been told by professionals? Was this commonly found within the autism population?

Questions I found myself unable to answer – but questions that spurred a burning desire to find out the answers; that desire is no less strong today as it was all those years ago. Since then I think my knowledge around how the sensory environment might impact autistic individuals has grown – while acknowledging that I have a vast amount to learn, so it was with great pleasure that I sat down to read this late one evening. I read the first chapter before I was told in no uncertain terms that it was bedtime. I went to bed smiling, knowing that I had the rest of the book to look forward to reading the following day!

In 2013, finally, sensory issues were included within one of the main diagnostic manuals in relation to autism. At last it seemed that the world in general was beginning to understand that traditional autism theory does not account for all things autistic! Sensory hyper and hypo sensitivities are becoming better understood – although there is clearly a long way to go.

Any information that gives society an insight into how an autistic person experiences life must be of some benefit; any information that allows a better understanding of how the sensory environment might play a part in those experiences is of potential value in a myriad of differing ways. What Sandra has done – in part through her having fallen in love with autoethnography – is exposed a part of her world to us readers. In my mind this is an astonishingly brave thing to do. Like so many other autistic adults who are proactively sharing their lives with the rest of the world, she is doing so with an openness and honesty that cannot, or should not, be overlooked. The number of blogs screaming out to be read, the autobiographical accounts, the autistic speakers at conferences and training events – the autistic voice – this should be the starting point for professionals and others on their own journey to a better understanding of autism. And yet this is so rarely the case. All over the globe autistic individuals are doing something so powerful, and doing it with an incredible selflessness, in sharing themselves with the world in such an open and honest way – and yet it seems so rare that it is understood for the extraordinary resource that it is. I am hopeful that Sandra's publication nudges more people along that road of discovery through an understanding that the real lived experience, presented to readers, is a gift that should never be turned down.

Sensory processing will impact each autistic person differently – and, indeed, one person's sensory experiences may differ from one day to the next, or even one minute to the next. Sandra makes this very clear – that autistic individuals are exactly that, individuals. However, this should not stop anyone from gaining insight through one person's experiences (well, two if you count Sandra's husband, who makes several 'guest' appearances throughout the book!). *Any* autistic experience is rich and to be learned from whenever possible. It's one of the things that should keep any autism professional firmly grounded, because every single autistic person can teach a professional something new – which means, unless one has met and learned from all autistic people, there is always more to learn – which is a delight, in my opinion.

One of the most anxious times in my professional life was when I inadvertently upset Sandra, to the point that she was considering whether she wanted to continue with me as her Doctoral supervisor; I am so relieved that the final decision came out in my favour. Not having Sandra in my life would leave a glaring hole.

What is the book about? Is it simply an autobiography? No. Is it a travel book? An autism theory book? A relationships book? A guidebook? A guidance book?

A guidance guidebook?! It is all of those things, and more. It's intriguing, it's compelling, and it's beautifully written. It holds a huge amount of information – some of it might be useful to autism professionals, some for parents, some for autistic readers (of course some readers might be autistic parents and professionals all at the same time!).

Above all, it's an informative, insightful, and a thoroughly enjoyable read.

Luke Beardon, Senior Lecturer in Autism,
Sheffield Hallam University

INTRODUCTION

If you imagine a city, you might at first think about the skyline, the buildings for which it is famous; you may then imagine cars zooming up and down, streets filled with dust and fumes, people crowded together on pavements, going in and out of buildings as they live and work in the city. Tourists might be among the bustle, taking photographs and choosing postcards to send home to their loved ones. The city can be challenging, and for many it is easier to walk around in a 'bubble', just getting to where you need to be without really appreciating what is all around you.

This book is a metaphorical 'window' into an autistic mind, a glimpse at how we see the world and, in this case, the city. We possess myriad sensory differences which alter our perspective of what we experience; sometimes we need the 'bubble', but at other times we live for the detail of the city around us.

You might get a sense of comfort from looking into this 'window', or new awareness, or simply a few tips that can be used when the city becomes too much. Whatever you take away, I hope you at least enjoy the read.

* * *

It is early afternoon on a summer's day. The streets are bustling with holidaymakers, workers, shoppers; around me, the buzz of chatter is rampant. I can feel the heat on my skin, and the aroma of the delicious heat makes me smile.

I have stopped to watch a street performer who is painted silver and appears to be sitting as still as a glorious statue in a museum. Unremarkable, you would think, but this silver man is suspended in mid-air without the apparent prop of a chair or table holding him upright. I am sure many of you have seen performers of this ilk and wondered what the secret is. Today there are people surrounding him, trying to put their hands around him, trying to solve the mystery of this seemingly floating human. I think I have worked out what may be happening, but I am unsure. Should I say something, ask him? I find myself getting frustrated and unable to hold back, and when the crowd leaves, I approach him and whisper my thoughts to him. He slowly nods and puts his finger to his mouth for me to stay silent. I put money in his hat on the ground and walk away, happy that I was right...and no, dear readers, I won't tell you his secret either.

Some people, it seems, are willing to respond to an honest and open individual, and are more trusting than many might think. It would have been considered inappropriate or socially unacceptable to ask this man his secret, but I have shown that sometimes it pays to be forthcoming. A trait very common in autistic individuals is this honesty and the need to say it as it is.

I have been 'blessed' with this trait since I was a child. Mostly, it came out at school; if I didn't want to be friends, I would usually say so. I was passionately obsessed with dancing and reading from the age of four, and if others didn't share those interests, I would deem them boring. I wasn't being rude in my mind, just honest. At the age of nine, I became very ill. Diagnosed with bone cancer and put through years of gruelling treatments, I continued to dance and read without really being overly worried about the illness. I did, however, want to know every minute detail along the way; doctors or nurses couldn't touch me unless I knew exactly what was about to happen. I found out many years later that as a child I was also extremely bossy towards other children, my parents and siblings, doctors…and, to be honest, I am probably still that way, although I try to rein it in. I don't consider it bossiness, but the need for control. If I don't feel in control of any situation, I panic or get extremely anxious. This is another trait for many autistic individuals, although in some it can result in frustration or anger to extreme levels rather than just bossiness.

After the five-year all-clear, life continued, but as I went into my teenage years I became ill again – arthritis this time. There were also lots of side effects from the cancer, but I just got on with things. I wanted to be good at whatever I did and nothing was going to stop me.

I have had a long business career, from the NHS to the Prison Service, in audit, administration, training and sports governance. I have been self-employed and freelance for more than 20 years, working in various sectors. During that time I have studied, trained as a teacher, achieved degrees and a doctorate. Illness and, as it turned out, autism have never stopped me.

I have never been afraid to tell people what I have gone through, what I have experienced; when I began to teach dance, and later business, teacher training and karate, I always talked about myself and used my experiences as examples of good and bad practice or to teach children about diversity in its varying forms.

My research and writing, past and present, is very firmly embedded in the methodology of autoethnography, a form of ethnography favoured and promoted by researcher and professor of communication and sociology at the University of South Florida, Carolyn Ellis, in her seminal 'novel' *The Ethnographic I* (2004). I fell in love with autoethnography while I was undertaking doctoral research; I liked the coincidence of having the same name, but having read a couple of essays about her work, I just felt inspired and knew this was the style of writing that was right for me, the premise being about putting the researcher into the research, or in this case the writer into the writing.

The only danger for me with this type of writing is that I can get carried away and words just flow from my brain – that same brain that doesn't filter and is a bit muddled. Of course, I can edit what comes out of my brain, but I am hoping you will forgive what I consider is my honesty and candour and at times a jumble of words – a bit like 'alphabet-spaghetti bolognese', with a little sauce and spice thrown in to 'make it taste better'. I make no apologies for this bizarre analogy and others which will no doubt follow. Comparing experiences to movies, television shows or music is another of my peculiar propensities. I really believe that I am more easily influenced by these because growing up was not easy as an autistic individual, feeling that I did not fit in at school or other social surroundings, and I watched and listened to whomever seemed to be popular role models.

My clinical diagnosis of Asperger's Syndrome was given when I was 43, after years of working with autistic individuals and in the midst of my doctoral research into the learning experiences of such individuals.

SENSING THE CITY

Whatever the reason you have picked up this book, I appreciate that you did and welcome you to my world. The concept came to me while I was on a city break with my husband. We were walking through a market and I was assaulted with vibrant colours, myriad sounds, and wonderful aromas of spices, food and hot cinnamon doughnuts. I could hear the bells of a local church as well as the sounds of the market, and I wondered, if I was not autistic, would I be so aware of what was around me or would I simply be looking for a new jacket or a gift for an aunt?

You may know nothing about autism and wonder how our perspective might be different; or you might be autistic or have a connection to autism and just be interested in what I have to offer. Whoever you are or whatever your reason for reading this, I hope not to disappoint. I am simply offering my perspective of what I consider to be an interesting topic, and if I manage to raise your autism awareness or leave you with a few life 'tools' which work for me, I have achieved success.

I consider myself to be mostly a very positive person. I try to see the good in every situation; I try to stay calm when something goes wrong and work my way through problems carefully and slowly until a solution shows itself. Don't get me wrong; though; often inside I am a bundle of anxiety, I get stomping great 'butterflies' in my stomach, I feel nauseous and talk to myself constantly. I have learned ways to *cope* in most circumstances. That in itself is frustrating to me: that we feel obliged to learn to *cope* – surely just *coping* is not living a fulfilled and happy life – surely we deserve more. I have been on a mission over the past couple of years to do more than *cope*: to have the best life for not only me but my family and friends. I have no intention of looking back when I am in my nineties and being glad I managed to just *cope* with my life.

I travel around many cities in the course of my life. Often it is to city universities to teach or participate in meetings, sometimes to speak at or present research to conferences or on training courses, or as a representative of professional organisations of which I am a member.

Sometimes it is simply to enjoy life, to have a holiday, to visit cultural institutions, meet friends or to shop. Whatever the reason I am visiting a city, I try to take the opportunity to make the most of what I experience, while at the same time not taking in so much that some of my more challenging autistic traits are brought to the surface in a bid to ruin my fun!

The chapters that follow cover many areas of experiencing and sensing a city. I have attempted to share my experiences with you in vast detail, as well as sometimes bringing in comparison experiences with other autistic individuals, including my husband who also has a clinical diagnosis of autism. Most individuals I mention shall remain nameless; some have had a diagnosis, others have not but follow and experience the patterns and traits minus the official 'stamp of autism'. I have covered areas including travelling to and around cities, eating (which I love to do), entertainment, which includes cultural and performance-related experiences, staying in cities, and living, which encompasses everything from keeping fit to having a latte in the park, visiting hospital or simply shopping – all of which I do on a regular basis. I have also added ideas along the way, which work for me; they are not specific to particular cities, just suggestions for when you are feeling the inevitable overload and are too overwhelmed to think straight.

I have kept chapters mostly short and choppy in a bid not to overload you as a reader. I love to read, but I favour dipping in and out of non-fiction books, and I find that much easier to do if chapters are kept shorter. It also helps to revisit a particular section if you want to, later on. I add quotations from time to time; I love a quotation, especially if it is from someone who inspires me or from a book I love to read.

My intention is not to tell you what to do in similar situations or to patronise; this is my perspective and sometimes that may not suit your way of thinking or living. I would ask that you remain open-minded and take from the book anything that you consider might be useful or inspirational. Of course, if you wish to use it alongside your city guide book, feel free to do so; nothing would make me happier as a writer.

For readers who are unfamiliar with autism, I have chosen to start with a chapter introducing the basics, but especially focused on sensory issues surrounding autism. I have attempted to explain in brief why our perspective may be different from the non-autistic city dweller, how autism can affect us on a daily basis, how we are all very different in the same way that one non-autistic individual is different from another.

For those readers in the know, please be patient while I take another step forward in the bid to raise autism awareness.

'The real voyage of discovery consists not in seeking new landscapes, but in having new eyes.'

Marcel Proust

At the start of one journey on my way to a new city, I encountered a group of young school children travelling to a local castle, just two train stops away. I watched and listened as they became more and more excited while waiting for the train to arrive. One little boy with a mohican hairstyle had apparently never even been on a train before and was bombarding the accompanying adults with questions about the train and the castle. His little face was alight with excitement and he couldn't get his words out fast enough. It was lovely to watch him and the other children getting so excited. I am sure most people sitting at that railway station would have completely ignored the group, and many would have just thought they were loud and annoying. How sad that they might have missed this opportunity to see the happiness and excitement exuding from these young people.

One wonders whether sensing a city from an autistic perspective is akin to a child's perspective: wondering how things work, what you will see, and asking questions... lots of questions.

I hope my perspectives give you some worthwhile answers.

CHAPTER 1

MAKING SENSE OF AUTISM

At intervals throughout this book, I shall be writing about 'autistic days'. I should explain right off what I mean by this for readers who have never experienced this phenomenon.

Do you have days when everything seems to go wrong? The alarm doesn't go off, you are late for work, the train breaks down, your sandwich has gone soggy, it rains and your hair goes wild...well, an autistic day can affect you in the same way, but it might take just one thing to cause it. It might be as small as the post being five minutes later than usual, or the teabags running out just as you need to make a cup of tea. Just one small thing can turn the day into a complete disaster: a diversion on your normal route to work or someone arriving a few minutes late for an appointment. These simple occurrences might spark the most disastrous and stressful day you could ever imagine. There will possibly be one or, more likely, most of the following: anger, tears, feelings of depression, anxiety, shouting, screaming, throwing things, overeating or not eating at all... The list is endless and quite extreme, but when you are caught up in one of these days, it just goes on for ever and makes you feel like nothing will help.

Sometimes the effects of an 'autistic day' can last for several days afterwards. Autistic individuals do not want sympathy, though; we also have spectacular days when our sensory differences, unique characteristics and abilities are put to good use and light us up inside.

One of the diagnostic differences for autistic individuals is that we are likely to have impairments in one or more of our senses. These impairments are more about perception than biological in nature such as blindness or deafness. An added complexity is that no two autistic individuals are likely to have the same sensory perceptual pattern. Whereas I might be affected by strong aromas, another might not even notice them at all. Some individuals perceive visually in small fragments rather than looking at a whole picture. My autistic husband often points out images in wallpaper, or on floor tiles, for example (apparently, we have a duck on our kitchen floor and Oliver Cromwell's face in our living room), whereas I can only see the overall differences in the natural slate and flowers on the wall.

We are assaulted with sensory stimuli from all directions and find it difficult to filter out information we don't need. In a restaurant, for example, a non-autistic person will listen to his fellow diner and be able to cut out most of the chatter going on around him. For an autistic person, this might not be possible; often he will have hyper-acute hearing and will be able to hear conversations all around the room, thus finding it difficult to focus on the voice of his companion. As well as conversations, he will likely hear other sounds: the clattering of cutlery, a telephone ringing, a child crying, a police siren outside, and even a bell from a serving hatch calling a waiter to the kitchen to collect meals (the latter heard by me just this morning). I was once teaching a karate class of children and could hear two parents in conversation across the room. I stopped the class and asked one of the parents a specific question relating to his conversation. He was shocked to say the least…and very embarrassed.

There are many theories relating to autism. Among them is the Gestalt perception theory which identifies an inability to separate foreground and background stimuli (Bogdashina, 2016). Weak central coherence theory (Frith, 2003) determines that the individual focuses more on the detail of something rather than appreciating it as a whole or putting it into an overall context. This theory is often blamed for an autistic individual not being able to see optical illusions – a chalk drawing on a pavement which depicts a large river, for example. Most non-autistic people will see the river and walk around it even though it is simply a chalk drawing. If an autistic individual has weak central coherence, in theory he should ignore the illusion and just walk across the pavement as normal. I would certainly walk around the river, especially given my abnormal fear of most things water-related, and drowning in particular. I have a particular passion for a piece of optical illusion artwork which hangs in the British Library in London. While I love the detail and get lost in it, I also love the illusion it creates and could happily stare at it for hours.

Paradoxically, we see everything in detail, but putting it all together into a holistic picture can often lead to sensory overload. The filters in our brains are filled with 'holes' which let far too much information in. This overload means that we are unable to select what we actually need or what is relevant, and we progress quickly to sensory meltdown, which is widespread panic causing diverse emotions and physical reactions. Meltdowns can be devastating both inwardly and in the way the individual lashes out. Meltdowns can be angry, depressive, verbally or physically aggressive, and mostly distressing. We often blank out what we do or say – it is not personal to anyone other than us – and we have usually been building up to it over hours, days or even weeks. Just one trigger can set it in motion, and sensory overload is a substantial trigger. Yes, that noisy toddler in the supermarket might just be autistic and having a meltdown... A more understanding world would be nice at times.

Even though I may not always progress to full overload, often if there are too many sensory triggers around me, I may just 'blank out'. This happens to me often when I am with other people; I can be chatting away one minute, and the next I just go completely silent; the chatter or noise around me goes over my head and I lose all focus. Outwardly, it looks as though I am ignoring people or I appear bored or rude. I just zone out. My internal system seems to just suddenly kick back in when my brain has caught up with everything it has digested. Not every autistic individual will react like this; we are a heterogeneous community of people and all have our own way of reacting or dealing with what happens to or around us.

Theory is essential, especially to advanced research, but it is sometimes easy to get caught up in it and forget the human 'subjects' of the research. Perception is complicated and, of course, subjective. We must continue to remember that no two autistic individuals are alike and they will all perceive their experiences in different ways. There are plenty of excellent researchers and writers who give outstanding theoretical perspectives and I would not wish to step into their genre of expertise.

I like to write about autism from my heart primarily, and along the way my head engages to put things into a theoretical context to satisfy my varied audience. The experiences in this book are explained in the way I perceive them; to others, with or without autism, they may seem odd or irrelevant to sensory perception, but to me it is all relevant. My thoughts come out of my head in a way that is unique to me, and I hope that you will be patient and open-minded as you read. Perhaps something I say will cause you to stop and reflect.

In an attempt to avoid repetitive description of autism theory in relation to sensory perception throughout the chapters of experiential perspectives, I shall encapsulate theoretical characteristics here which are likely to affect my sensing a city, thus putting the experiences into clearer context.

Sensory perception, especially as it relates to autism, is about much more than the five senses of sound, smell, sight, touch and taste. It is about the following:

- Experiencing differences in temperature (thermoception) – for example, extremes in feeling hot or cold are common.

- Difficulties with balance and proprioception – these often include poor sense of direction, a lack of awareness of personal body placement and movement, resulting clumsiness, lack of coordination and bumping into things. For example, I currently have a huge bruise on my ankle due to repeatedly hitting it on the corner of the open dishwasher door.

- Pain or extreme discomfort with day-to-day activities – for example, cutting hair or toenails, or wearing certain fabrics. For some it is a hug or light touch or breath on the skin that is intolerable (hypertactility). Many strip off clothes at the first opportunity as the fabric is creating extreme reactions.

- Not experiencing pain when you usually would expect to (hypotactility) – boiling water, for example.

- Internal sensation and perception within the mind (Ayatana); this is a Buddhist concept. An example might be perceiving information in another form – seeing words as pictures or sounds as colours.

- Hearing quiet sounds on 'high volume' – for example, the buzz of a refrigerator or a fluorescent light (hyper-hearing).

- Issues with food tastes, smells and textures being intolerable. Often this is related to colour. For instance, I can't eat foods which are red (except for tomato-based foods). They remind me of a chemotherapy drug I was given as a child and, strangely, I equate the food and drug taste simply because of the colour. Sometimes it can be a difference in food brand which causes anxiety.

- How individuals experience visual perception. Some individuals wear long sleeves so that they know exactly where their arm ends, or run their hands around the edge of something to get perspective of its shape or where a piece of furniture is in the room.

- A necessity to taste something simply to confirm what it is or because they like the texture: grass, rubber or, my favourite as a child, ice. I remember scraping the ice build-up in the freezer box into a cup to eat, without my mum's knowledge. It was comforting and felt good on my tongue.

- Repeated movements for an extended period without dizziness or nausea (vestibular hypo-sensitivity). This is often rocking, swaying or spinning. I often get a dance move stuck in my head and I can spend 30 minutes or more doing it while I am watching television, or in a queue, or in fact anywhere. I find it to be therapeutic.

- A need to touch what is seen – texture is extremely important.

- Certain actions: peeling things, breaking a seal on a coffee jar, stroking textures…

It is clear from this list that there are many sensory issues that may affect autistic individuals; the list is not exhaustive and, importantly, may not apply to everyone with an autism diagnosis. For those people who do not experience these sensations, it is difficult to understand them, but they are very real and can be very distressing, or indeed reassuring, for the autistic individual who does experience them. An abundance of sensory stimulation can cause the individual great anxiety, but paradoxically can also be a great comfort if it is the right stimulation for that individual.

I have always maintained that autistic individuals are people of extremes. I am not always comfortable in simple social situations, such as meeting a small group of people for the first time, yet I am happy to dance on stage in front of hundreds or thousands of strangers. I can be on a high and excitable one moment, and in seconds can become quiet and withdrawn for no explicable reason. We often seem to be able to change reaction as quickly as if someone had flicked a switch or pressed a button.

From a sensory point of view, as I have described, autistic individuals can be either hyposensitive or hypersensitive to certain triggers, and in some cases both. I may be able to repeat a particular action for a long time without negative effect, but ask me to spin around or jump up and down and the outcome will be quite different. I am very coordinated when I dance or perform karate moves, but throw me a ball to catch or ask me to navigate a room with lots of furniture and my coordination leaves me in an instant. I am constantly bruised, a state I actually don't mind because I love to watch the bruises change colour – an appeal shared by other autistic people, apparently. This fascination is useful these days as I love yoga and my coordination and balance is still challenging for me at times. I also struggle more than most with certain postures which involve wrapping arms and legs in different directions; they just confuse me.

It may sound as though autism is a negative condition, and certainly if you listen to much of what is spoken about it in the media, you may have this opinion. There are certainly negative aspects and, depending on where on the autism spectrum an individual is, these can be extreme in many cases. For those of us on the so-called higher functioning end of the spectrum, life is not always so great, despite outward appearances. We all have anxieties, uncertainties and meltdowns. I can be sitting on a train, trapped by the smells around me. If someone comes on to the train and is wearing a particularly strong perfume, I have nowhere to go. The perfume may cause headaches, my face to burn and my breathing to labour, but if I moved into a different carriage, how could I be sure that there was not another smell that might be even stronger or more painful than the first?

There are ways, though, that our very existence is an 'ideal'. Who wouldn't want to speak their mind, no matter what? Surely we would all love to see details, intricate colours, tantalising textures… My acute sense of detail and extreme sense of passion and focus has made me a successful business woman in a variety of work areas. I have a determination to thrive, rather than simply *cope*, and to have a wonderful time doing what I love without feeling I have to justify my abilities or, in the words of Wenn Lawson, 'diff-abilities' (2011). I agree with him entirely, preferring 'differences' to 'difficulties'.

Language is a whole other issue and not one I will be discussing, except to say that throughout this book I have used 'autistic individual' rather than 'individual with autism' as some would advocate. This is personal preference as I believe autism is part of me and not an add-on. I do not wish to offend anyone with this choice. I also use the term 'autist' from time to time. Again, it is my preference to use this term rather than more popular terms of 'autie' and 'aspie', both of which I personally dislike. Lastly, I use the term 'non-autistic' rather than 'neurotypical'. I prefer this, and for readers who are not autistic I believe it is a more kindly term.

* * *

And so let me take you on a sensory journey, into my world… In the words of Atticus Finch, 'You never really understand a person until you consider things from his point of view…until you climb inside of his skin and walk around in it' (Lee, 1960).

GETTING AROUND

'It is better to travel well than to arrive.'

Buddha

CHAPTER 2

STREETWISE

I love to walk around a city, especially when I am alone, ambling along at my own pace, observing and listening to what is going on around me. On a practical level, it is much safer to be aware of my environment as I walk, but it is so much more than that for me. By walking, especially if I am in a new area or new city, my senses are open to what is around me and I can get a feeling for the place. It also helps me to know where I am geographically; if I used an underground train to get around all the time, I would never know where I was in relation to other places. It is not easy for me, though, to walk around, not knowing exactly where I am going; I get anxieties and, depending on my end destination and the reason for these anxieties, they can range from mild to shattering.

Of course, I could cycle and possibly get a similar experience. I am sure this is so for many who love the freedom of wheels in the open air, but cycling is not for me. My balance is terrible on a bicycle; I declared when I was eight years old that I would never cycle again after spending hours and hours trying to get some kind of balance. I realise I sound somewhat melodramatic, but in my opinion cities are far safer when I am on my own two feet and not wobbling around on two wheels! For this reason, some cities are to be visited with caution. A favourite of mine, Copenhagen, is one of the most stunning and clean I have seen, in part likely because the natives go pretty much everywhere by bicycle. For those of you who love a statistic, apparently fewer than 30 per cent of residents own a car. Happily, it is also full of character-filled narrow streets with cobblestones for me to walk along; the incredibly elaborate architecture is a sight to behold. For water lovers, there are myriad waterways weaving in and out of the city, creating a calm oasis among the ancient castles and palaces. As any autistic individual will tell you (if you don't already know), we love, and indeed need, a calm oasis wherever we happen to be. Regardless of which city I am in, I try to make it my number one research priority to find a few places I can go to for quiet respite when the inevitable sensory overload hits. Sometimes it might simply be a green area in which to sit or stand and just breathe deeply.

On a chilled shopping trip walking around the city, I might be mildly anxious; usually, there is no particular time schedule, no appointments, deadlines or specific places to be. My senses tend to be more open on these occasions. On a trip to a city for a purpose – a meeting, a conference to attend, a hospital appointment perhaps – my anxiety levels increase radically and I have a tendency to shut out everything around me. This is more a result of thoughts of finding a new place and having to be there by a certain time. I cannot control my environment, public transport or other people. My way of controlling these specific visits happens even before I leave my house, sometimes weeks before the event. The pre-trip preparation usually involves a lot of research, downloading maps and directions, as well as finding local restaurants, parks and hotels to which I can escape when overload hits me. I can spend hours and hours finding hotels which suit me; this involves checking out the local area to see if there are nearby shops, a supermarket, coffee shops I favour, the distance from the railway station, telephone numbers of taxi firms just in case, bus routes, and how the hotel is laid out so that

I know which rooms are near noisy roads, party rooms or the ice machine (I have added this last one since a recent trip to New York!). I love searching maps online to find the street views; I trace my whole journey from arrival in the city to the hotel, and then to wherever I want to go. It truly enrages me if I get to the location and find roadworks or a building has been changed. This all sounds bizarre to a non-autistic person, but I know many of you will identify with these almost obsessive plans and be chuckling to yourselves at this point.

If I am due to attend a function where I am expected to eat at a buffet with crowds of people, these escape plans are extremely useful; they avoid the social networking and eating-in-front-of-others scenario that I (and many other autists) loathe so much. I have even been known to arrive in a city and walk the exact route I will need to walk the following day to an appointment. I can then relax more and enjoy my surroundings.

One of my biggest fears when I walk around a city is bumping (literally, that is) into other people. With the increasing use of technology on the streets, including for directions and maps, people seem to always have their eyes staring at a screen rather than in front of them. Often they don't even notice when they bump into someone. I loathe touching strangers or them pushing or prodding me. This happens, I have noticed, often when waiting for lights to change colour, or when I am trying to cross the road, or I am near a store entrance. For my husband, this is a danger zone; if he is pushed by someone, however accidentally, it is likely to send him into overload, and his rage can go from 0 to 80 in a second. I have seen situations where crowds have sent him into near meltdown, and, of course, no one around him knows what is really happening. They just see an angry man in what seems to be an innocent situation.

Another panic point for me when I am trying to find a particular place is the ever-changing road system. A map, even an online one, may say one thing, and a week later the road is closed or a new one has been added. For autistic individuals who have researched thoroughly, this is likely to cause high anxieties. We do not always have the confidence to stop someone and ask where we should go. It would be easier, perhaps, simply to hail a taxi cab, as I discuss later in the chapter, but I feel both lazy and extravagant doing this too often.

However difficult it may be, walking around a city, mostly I love it. I love to people-watch, and I love the plethora of colours in the way people dress around the streets (although why must so many wear black?), the beautiful buildings, the posters and billboards declaring the latest must-haves or movies to see. I love to see wall art or graffiti: full of myriad colours, such beautiful detail whatever the subject, and a treat for the eyes. Regardless of whether you like what you see, or whether or not you agree with people painting on public buildings or walls, I am amazed by the incredible techniques of the artists. Even a simple word can show great skill and passion. Of course, all art is subjective, whether in an art gallery or on the side of a building. On summer days, I stare up at the sky – bright blue with divine fluffy white clouds creating images that I could watch all day. My senses are alive in the city; rainbows are my absolute favourite and I watch them intently for as long as possible. They fascinate me, the way the colours come together but are so distinct; it eludes me how the arc can be so perfect, seen from every angle in a slightly different way. This truly is one of nature's miracles. Along with rainbows, of course, comes the rain; I delight in the feeling and smell of fresh rain on a dry sunny day, as if it has been sent down to refresh everything.

I try to appreciate all that I see, all that I smell and all that I hear. I often get an itchy nose as people wearing strong perfumes pass me by, or watery eyes if I am passing a park or garden where flowers or grasses exude their strong but beautiful scents. Even though I may find them uncomfortable, they may be aromas that fill others with glee. Often I will smile at someone walking past; he or she may seem vulnerable or sad, or simply be wearing an exquisitely coloured scarf or sweater. I love to look for detail in the seemingly unassuming: a lad's fantastically wild afro hairstyle, school children talking excitedly, rows of perfect fruit on a street stall...

Not all cities are created equal, but each and every one has its own personality, its quirks and uniqueness, the reasons people choose to visit them. For autistic individuals, each city will also have its challenges, and I cannot emphasise enough how important it is to research so that you know what to expect. There are some cities, in Asia in particular, I would love to visit, but research warns me I would find them more challenging and preparation might need to be more focused. If I desperately wanted to visit, though, autism would not stop me; I would just need to find a way to feel safe and comfortable as far as possible. It might be that I would need to travel with someone who knew the area, who had travelled there often and who I could put my trust in. I might just need a tour guide in the city, or to stay in a particular area which would make me feel more secure. I find there are always ways around my difficulties if I look hard enough. That is probably not the case for all autistic individuals and no one should feel under any pressure to be in a situation if it is too uncomfortable.

Some cities are gargantuan, where everything seems to be scaled up. Christmas movies (which I adore) seem to focus on such cities, and New York in particular is one which I love, but find difficult in some ways. I am always amazed, though, at the size of everything: from the buildings to the road widths; if I viewed it from the air, people would be little ants moving quickly between buildings. One of my favourite aspects of this city and other major cities in the USA is the way the roads are based on a grid system, with streets going from east to west and seemingly endless avenues going from north to south. With this system alone, I feel so much safer as it is relatively easy to find my way around. I have even been stopped for directions and been able to give them. This system gives me the confidence to walk into areas I don't know and explore, as I am not afraid of getting lost or feeling vulnerable as I look at a map.

The disadvantage for autistic individuals, though, might just be the increased size of everything, and the sheer volume of people, traffic, buildings and so on. Sensory overload can be quick to come, as a big city can be extremely tiring; there are colours, sirens, car horns, bright lights, noise simply everywhere. It must be tiring for anyone, but for autists the tiredness can be off the scale. I always leave inspired and enthused, but tired beyond belief. These city breaks are limited to a few days only for my husband and me now. We simply can't cope with any longer; our senses are fit to burst – and that is before the long journey home by air and road. Home is definitely our safe haven.

We have found, however, like most other cities anywhere, there are respite areas and quieter streets, often just one block away from the chaos and buzz of tourists and traders loudly selling their goods. There are also many green areas: parks in the middle of the city, where there are often chairs and tables set up near little refreshment huts. In the summer, there are people lounging around on rugs, sunbathing or reading, getting their own respite from the craziness of city life. Bigger parks offer their communities free concerts and entertainment at all times of the day. For the brave autist who has relaxation tools up his or her sleeve (not literally, of course), cities such as this are exhilarating places to be. Be prepared to sleep well as tiredness can hit quickly and suddenly.

In any city, I find my frame of mind and how I react to sensory stimulants depend very much on the time of day, time of year even, or where I am heading. Rush hour can cause acute anxiety, but is also interesting if, for example, I am sitting in a park watching others rushing about. If I have lots of time, I can enjoy every sensation as I walk around, taking them all in as I wander. If I have a particular place to go by a particular time, however, and I am in a more anxious state of mind, every sensory experience can be pure torture. Smells can be abundant: diesel fumes, the smell of curry from an Indian restaurant, someone with strong perfume passing by, or a flower stall – usually wonderful, but on this kind of day the mix of floral aromas is just too much.

If walking among the streets and crowds is too much for you suddenly, you could always call a taxi cab. I love to ride a taxi cab from time to time. I have been known to get so overwhelmed in a city that I just give up and hail a cab. It is my equivalent of a child who has a tantrum and just sits down in the middle of the pathway refusing to move (I admit I did this as child). I can relax and enjoy watching the city around me as I am slowly driven to my destination. My biggest stressor is hailing a cab to start with. The way this is done will depend on the city, but I have a few tips to make it a little easier:

- Try not to hail a taxi cab around the time of shift changeover; the drivers are usually in a rush to go off duty and they may refuse the fare if the journey takes them out of their way. Research in each city is useful to find out these times, which are generally standard and detailed on websites and in guide books.

- Each city will have places where it is easier to hail a cab; sometimes there are even specific queues with attendants taking your destination to give to the cab driver for you.

- Stand on the right side of the road for the direction you want to travel (if you know which way that is, of course); it saves the taxi cab turning around or wasting your money and time by driving up and down roads to avoid one-way systems.

- Be aware of how signs in the cabs work: whether the light should be on or off if it is free, if there is an available sign. This saves a lot of wasted time and frustration, and thus avoids anxiety or anger if you are already close to overload or in meltdown.

If I am to travel a short distance and the weather is fine enough, I have been known to call a cycle rickshaw. I believe in some parts of Asia these electric taxi equivalents are called tuk-tuks because of the sound they make. I love the way I feel part of the city in one of these. At times I can feel vulnerable, but I strangely trust the rider in charge; it is in his or her interest to keep me safe. I love that I am driven around streets I wouldn't normally venture along, the secret passages of a city only usually known by the natives. I've discovered many lovely places along the various journeys I've taken. I've noticed interesting buildings, hidden gems of stores I will go back to, wonderful aromas of street vendors cooking food from around the world.

I am always in a good mood in a cycle rickshaw; I tend to smile and wave to passers-by who often wave back. It makes me feel like a child and able to be a little bit cheeky. Many of the riders have fantastic customer service. In New York, for instance, my husband and I met a completely whacky charismatic rider who stopped at every traffic light (and in Manhattan there are many) and told us jokes and stories. He interacted with members of the public walking by and, if I am honest, probably annoyed far too many drivers; for us as customers, though, the experience was exhilarating and fun. With all the wonderful experiences, of course, comes the impact of autistic differences. As we near main roads, I get anxious about being mowed down by taxi cabs rushing around doing their jobs. Some smells which are not so good come from the extremely close proximity of the car and bus exhausts; a scarf is useful at these times, to pull a little higher. If you happened to be riding one during a more stressful time, it may cause sensory overload. But with the right frame of mind, it can be simply wonderful.

Last but not least is the bus. In some cities, they are long and bendy; others may be open-topped and full of tourists or small and compact. Although I quite enjoy a bus ride, watching out of the window at the city passing me by, I get anxious about what to do, how to pay, where to sit, how to get off. All these questions go through my head when I think about getting one, so usually I don't. If someone travels on one daily, then these questions are not relevant and they become a stress-free way to travel. I also worry that I might be forced to sit next to an over-aromatic person, be trapped by passengers standing very close, or not know where to get off. As my balance is not the best, I also worry I will be told to go upstairs and then not be able to get back down in time for my stop.

I am not sure I consider myself completely streetwise, but I am always keen to try new city streets...just not as spontaneously as the non-autistic person might. For me it takes time and a new level of courage.

CHAPTER 3

COME FLY WITH ME

I have a love–hate relationship with the experience of flying. I love the actual flying part mostly, but it is the experience around the periphery which causes the most difficulties: the airport, and even the preparation for the airport. I should clearly add that by flying I mean the normal large airplanes rather than the whole host of other flying objects people seem to subject themselves to: microlights, hot air balloons, sky diving, parachuting – madness in my opinion, although I am partial to a helicopter ride from time to time. Flying holds for me excitement and anticipation, but it is out of my control and therefore the unexpected aspects of flying also engender anxieties and confusion. There is plenty of opportunity for the senses to be completely overloaded, so planning is crucial.

Let's start with booking flights. Just this alone fills me with dread. Do I purchase online, which on the surface seems easier? No interaction, just find what I need and book. But it's not that simple, is it? There are a multitude of websites to choose from, and each has a different way of doing things, requirements to complete, and I admit I just get confused. For some reason, booking a flight seems a whole lot more serious than booking a rail ticket. Of course, many flights are more expensive than a train journey, but it is the number of options to choose which has me frazzled. Even if I look at the diagram of the inside of the airplane with its seats, I have no idea which way faces the front. When I flew to New York recently, I expected our seats to be in the back row, but they were in fact in the front row. This might give us more leg room, but it also means people try to cut through this row to visit the loos on either side. The saving grace was the couple next to us with a baby so a bassinette (a portable cradle) was attached to the wall in front which blocked the passage. I never thought having a baby next to us on a flight would be an advantage!

Usually, I opt to call eventually, just so that I can ask myriad questions before letting the person take my credit card details. It all seems so final and scary. When they email the paperwork, I must check the details a hundred times or more; I promise you, this is no exaggeration. In the weeks or even months leading up to the flight, I probably check them several times a week at least. The day of travelling, I check my bag at least 20 times to look at my passport and tickets (or e-tickets on my phone) to confirm in my mind that they are there. It is utterly exhausting to be honest, but doing this is really out of my control.

On my last flight, despite all this checking, I realised the day before we were due to fly home that I had got it in my head that our flight was at 7pm when in actual fact it was 9pm. The anxiety this sudden change in our plans caused was unrelenting until the flight actually left the airport. This, mixed in with other factors in a busy airport, so very late at night, resulted in a flight best left in the past. We were so glad to get home on that occasion and both vowed never to fly again. The problem is that anxieties are increased to such a high level when the senses are overloaded. Airports have bright lights, lots of often unexplained noises, tired and excited people, a variety of smells, and uncertainty.

Adding my husband into the mix when I am flying, and my stress levels are raised to more than 100 per cent (if that was actually possible). He hates to fly, and also hates the airport experience.

Although I find airports confusing and I get anxious, if I am alone and I have plenty of time, I can get through the experience relatively calmly… Not when I am with my husband, though. I am happy to take longer than most to go through the process, whereas he will want to get through it as quickly as possible. If he could afford to, he would only ever fly by private plane, where everything was organised for him and he was just taken from airport to airplane without any aggravation. We can only dream!

I have experienced many city airports including Gatwick, Heathrow, Stansted, Edinburgh, Glasgow, New Jersey, New York, Miami, Belfast, Copenhagen, Helsinki… They all vary in size, but their main purpose, of course, is to enable travellers to see the world for various reasons. This is truly an incredible reason for existing. They are not just about travelling, though; many have become destinations: to meet people, to shop, to eat and drink, to fall in love (if you believe in the movies), even to relax and have a massage, as well as to conduct business meetings. This is why the travelling experience is far more complex than just checking in and boarding an airplane, and why the practice becomes more stressful for an autistic individual.

No longer can we go through security (full of anxieties in itself) and straight to the boarding gate. Instead, we have to weave in and out of duty-free counters, and crowds of people trying to snap up a bargain, which in my opinion is probably not so much of a bargain anyway. Why buy things before you travel when they just have to be carried back and forth? However, when I am travelling alone, I do love to sit and watch other people. I wonder where they are going: a lovely holiday, a foreign wedding, a work trip, retreat, or even to live. I always have an eye on the boards detailing each flight and whether mine might be boarding yet. At all times, I know exactly where the next place is I need to be, so I never relax until I am sitting in my seat on the airplane, minus the horribly itchy blanket that all airlines seem to provide.

Finally we make it to what has to be the worst part of flying for me: security! As I revealed in the Introduction, I have had many illnesses; resulting surgeries have left a fair bit of metal inside me. Beeping, scanning and a pat-down are par for the course when I fly. Although the privacy is not so great, I prefer the newer-style X-ray machines as they save time and the humiliating experience of standing legs akimbo while a stranger proceeds to pat me all over in front of a queue of people. Perhaps as autistic individuals, it would be useful to wear some kind of lanyard so that security staff know we might object to such random touching. If any airport staff are reading this, perhaps you might kindly suggest this to your bosses? Other than the actual walk through, I am extremely organised: my liquids are already in a see-through zipped bag, my phone and tablet are ready to be extracted from my lightweight carry-on tote, and my pockets are emptied. I don't wear a belt to fly, my shoes are slip-on, my jacket is always off and ready. If in doubt, you should check out *Up in the Air*, a George Clooney (swoon!) movie, in which he plays a frequent flyer and demonstrates this process perfectly. I took notice; we autists take many cues from movies and watching others. Tip: wear socks with shoes unless you want the feeling of a dirty floor under your feet and the chance of catching a foot disease.

Despite getting anxious, I try to concentrate on the activity of the moment rather than what will happen. This is not easy, but there are stress points that I try to anticipate and find a solution for:

- getting to the airport early
- checking in bags (I try not to for short-haul flights)
- getting through security
- getting through the correct gate on time
- getting through security at the destination, especially after an international flight, which can be extremely anxiety-ridden and confusing to me
- finding any checked-in bag at the destination
- getting from the airport to hotel or home.

Apart from these stressors, I try to enjoy the experience as much as possible, taking in all the sights, sounds and smells in a more positive way, even learning tips from watching how other people seem to breeze through the process, ready for use on the next flight.

Now, when it comes to the actual flight, I am usually in my element. Even if my seat is not ideal, I try to make the most of the experience. For me, it is always worth paying a little more if I am in a position to do so, to sit in a slightly upgraded and larger seat. Last-minute free upgrades are not so frequent with the more popular online check-in. Also, I get panicky if I am sitting in a row where I am squeezed between strangers; it can be so claustrophobic. It is worth mentioning autism at the time of booking; this can make a difference to where you are seated. This is not so easy when booking online, though.

As for many people, taking off and landing are not my favourite parts of a flight. I never look out of the window (I prefer the aisle seats anyway for easy access), and I generally close my eyes or use a meditation application on my phone with earbuds, to close off the noise and vibrations. I use this when I am trying to sleep as well, so if you struggle to relax, you might want to check this out; there are plenty of different ones to suit everyone.

Once I am in my seat, I enjoy organising my little domain with my comfort items: book, lip balm (essential wherever I am), notebook and pencil, earbuds and phone. I read the obligatory magazine, planning my movie watching or what I might buy in Duty Free (most of which I neither want nor need). I have a cute little eye mask which I rarely wear as I don't often sleep on flights, but every list for travelling contains an eye mask so it must be important. If a published list tells me something is needed, I have tendency to believe it; I have with me the prerequisite ear plugs, toothbrush, snooze pillow, pashmina and so on. I go for a walk every hour and drink lots of water. I get excited by airplane food (I know what you may be thinking: yes, I am a bit strange), but always carry the recommended nuts and seeds, being careful to leave them on the airplane in case the country I am travelling to doesn't allow them to be brought in.

I enjoy everything about a flight. I love to watch the airline staff walk up and down the aisles helping passengers, with a permanent smile on their faces. I dreamed about being a flight attendant once, but I knew they had to be able to swim and this put me off. The thought of wearing the special uniform and walking through the airport with a suitcase was exciting. Yes, looking back, being with people all day long, with nowhere to escape, would have probably been a nightmare for me. Actually, I am not keen on the loos either, so on second thoughts… The thought of all those people using just a few loos; let's face it, a toilet is a vessel sat on (mainly) by strange bottoms, one of the most intimate parts of a human body. No one usually cleans it after each use, so it really is a quite a strange thing, don't you think?

Bottoms aside, I shall remain a grateful passenger enjoying the experience of in-flight food and entertainment, caught up in my own little world. Where shall I go next?

LONDON TO NEW YORK: AUTISTIC DIFFERENCES

This case study gives an overview of a flight taken to New York with my husband recently. It highlights the trigger points and how a dual-autistic couple handle a flight so differently and react to each other's anxieties and sensory differences.

- I had booked a taxi to take us to Heathrow, but I was anxious about whether it would arrive on time. Joe loathes anyone or anything to be later than expected, and it would cause a meltdown if the taxi was even five minutes late. Phew, it was early, and – relief – the driver was really lovely. I could relax...at least for most of the drive. In the airport vicinity, he didn't follow the usual route to our terminal; I panicked a little, but he explained it was a taxi-driver shortcut.

- We had arrived early...surely time to relax? No. Looking around was too much already. Too many people. Too many signs. Too many bright lights.

- We walked through the main doors...and the questions began: which desk, can we drop our bags, have you checked in? I needed time to get my bearings and find out where we needed to go; Joe expected me to know instantly. My anxiety levels had begun to rise.

- 'Ask someone, I need to relax.' 'What did she say?' 'Oh, great, come on then, let's do it, where do we line up?' He practically ran to a queue while I was trying to juggle the paperwork out of my bag. He threw the case on the roller incorrectly and then got annoyed when told he needed to put it the right way around. He was busy cracking inappropriate anecdotes when the staff member was telling him what to do. I hoped we weren't going to get taken away by security. I was relieved when that part was over with.

- 'Where now?' Upstairs, and I was happy to get a drink and relax a little. No… 'Let's just get through security.' I needed time to empty my water bottle, put passports away and get liquids ready. Before I knew it, we were in the security queue. 'What do I need to take off? Do I need to take my tablet out of my bag, shoes off?' The sign says take laptops out… 'This is not a laptop.' Everything was in the bins, and he went through security. Security staff wanted the tablet out, so I was left dealing with this while he waited impatiently at the other side. Having sorted the bins for both of us, I eventually walked through and the beeping began… I was left to get everything out of the bins, and while I was trying to get dressed again, he was walking into the airport lounge searching for the way out of Duty Free, which was packed. He walked into people and was getting really stressed. The lights were 'burning his head' and the noise was clearly getting to him. I finally found a corner table in a café where he could sit and get his tablet out and calm down.

- We had booked a more private lounge, so once we had arrived there, he relaxed for the first time. We had a meal, and then I went back into the main lounge to look around and get a sense of what was about.

- The plane was boarding and he wanted to wait until the last minute to walk to the gate, but I was anxious so we compromised and waited a little. He was right;

there was a delay and there were people everywhere. We had to wait, standing up, for an hour – people all around us were noisy, fed-up, and it was hot, so very hot. I could see by the look on his face that he was so close to overload and I worried about what he might do if we didn't board soon. Once everyone else started to board, we hung back and were the last people to get on the flight. He had extra leg room and no seats in front so he relaxed to a degree, which meant I could relax.

- The flight wasn't stress-free; a child behind was sick, he couldn't get his television screen to work, it was incredibly hot, and there was a woman who continually tried to squeeze past him to get to the toilet by an unconventional route, which angered him.

- We reached JFK Airport, though. At customs, it got worse: automatic check-in screens which were confusing, having to queue anyway as the screen couldn't read my fingerprints, delays and taking too long, lack of sleep (by then it was halfway through the night in the UK), freezing cold, couldn't find the taxi queue, and then we had to check in at the hotel.

On the way home there was an issue with online booking which managed to separate us in the airplane. We succeeded in sitting either side of the aisle in the same row eventually, but the problem caused extreme anxieties and was only resolved by kind passengers.

If you are autistic, you will no doubt recognise many of these trigger points; if not, you may find this quite baffling: how a process undertaken by millions of people each day of each year, all over the world, could cause such a high level of anxiety. This is autism!

CHAPTER 4

DERAILED

I am a regular train user and have travelled to and from various cities, mainly in the UK, over the years. The exceptions to this have been on the Subway system of New York City and on trams in Finland. I find train travel very satisfying and usually relaxing, although there have been occasions when travel has caused anxieties and sensory overload, mainly due to delays, cancellations or re-routes I was not expecting.

I love the freedom of driving, but after commuting by car for many years in and around cities, in my old 'employed' work life, I became exhausted by sitting in traffic jams and having to stay so switched on as to avoid being the victim either of accidents or of the inevitable 'road rage' which sadly accompanies busy roads. I work freelance now in many cities across the UK and abroad, and I travel by train often; it is usually my choice if I am travelling more than an hour or so. It allows me time: time to sit and do nothing, to watch and listen, to read or work, or simply to eat and drink while someone else is responsible for getting me to my destination safely and in most cases on time! It is remarkable how much goes on in a train if you open your senses up to it. Prior to researching this book, I travelled many journeys with my head stuck in a book or with headphones on, listening to music or podcasts, not noticing a thing except passengers sitting next to me, getting on and off the train, or the occasional passenger blessed with 'interesting' aromas.

For four years, I travelled 360 miles every six weeks to study at a university with an outstanding reputation for autism education, all by train. What started as an anxiety-ridden journey, with constant changes, unfamiliar surroundings and people, became a journey I mostly loved and one that I still miss years later.

Many of my train journeys are long ones, usually including overnight stays at my destinations. In this case, I will always book advance tickets so that I can ensure I travel facing the way I am going (to prevent travel sickness), in an aisle (to ensure easy access) or simply to guarantee a seat on a train to avoid uncertainty.

I get accustomed to particular railway lines, companies and trains; I have luggage that fits exactly under the aisle seat, and I have my favourite food outlets at well-used railway stations. In fact, I love railway stations; my husband, in contrast, sees them as anxiety inducers. There are certain exceptions to this lovefest, such as the time I was travelling to Manchester and all the trains were either delayed or cancelled due to flooding on the line. I was so panicked; I was due to teach on an autism course the morning after, and I had an advance ticket which was only valid on a particular train. After wandering around the station for what seemed like hours, speaking to various staff members, I made the decision to board the first train and hope that my ticket would be accepted. As it happened, it was the last one to leave that day. The station was literally full of people; by that, I mean the crowds were so packed together we were virtually touching. It was a scary experience for me; anxieties about not getting to my destination were enough, but add in the sensory issues: noises including continuous loud tannoy announcements, heat, lights, frantic people all around me, not enough space to breathe. That was a day I shall not forget in a hurry. Many other autists would have coped very differently, overload causing meltdown; I can imagine my husband would likely have become enraged with the overwhelming situation and become very distressed and angry even. Sudden rages are all too familiar in some autists' lives.

In city railway stations, especially if it is my first visit, I try to allow lots of time to explore, but also to feel comfortable that I will be able to catch my train on time without rushing about and getting anxious. Of course, I can't control other people and how their actions or words may affect me.

I never quite know how I will react to the unexpected. One day in London, I was going down an escalator to my train when I saw an elderly person fall on the upward escalator next to mine. Her bags spilled out and she started screaming. Someone immediately rushed to her aid, but I was so shocked by what I saw that I went into an unexplained mini-meltdown. I got to the bottom of the escalator and just stood and stared. I couldn't seem to move; my limbs felt as though they were made of concrete. Everyone walked around me, but I couldn't hear what was going on. Eventually, a member of staff came over and asked me if I was OK. This snapped me out of the state, but I relived that moment over and over for the rest of that day. Even now, several months later, I cannot forget the screams and the look of panic on her face.

I love to people-watch, so mainline stations are great places for that; I sit with a drink, watching and wondering about where and why people are travelling. One day I watched as a bird flew around in the station; I was mesmerised and watched it for at least ten minutes without even remembering where I was.

Sometimes, though, it just gets too much. I can be enjoying the experience one moment, and then the next I am so hot that I feel as if I am going to combust. I always carry water and a face spray just in case.

For the most part, I relax when I board the train, setting up my little area up with my comfort items as I do on an airplane (Chapter 3). Rather than read my book or listen to music, I have tried on more recent journeys to observe and listen more – to engage with the journey rather than cut myself off from it. Travelling on non-high-speed trains allows me to simply watch out of the window and connect in some way with nature or with urban life.

Gone are the days when passengers read or sleep; all around me, it seems, people set up laptops, switch on tablets and check their phones. The beeps, musical alerts and keyboard clicks are constant and quite annoying. I am always careful when I travel by train to turn off my alerts and technology beeps. I even put my phone to silent. Are these courtesies not a part of good public etiquette now? It seems not. On one occasion, I saw a passenger playing music videos on his tablet with no headphones plugged in, completely oblivious to the noise he (or, more accurately, his tablet) was making and to the fact that everyone around him was staring and tutting. While his focus was impressive, it was, in my opinion, at best rude and at worst extremely irritating.

So many voices are heard – some clear and loud as though they want everyone on the train to hear their conversations, others muffled and whispered. I hear so many loud conversations on mobile phones. If I am in the right mood, I can become fascinated by the conversations; if I am feeling anxious or overwhelmed, these can be infuriating and lead to too much information taking over my brain. Why do people have such private conversations in a public place, I wonder. I once heard someone give out their credit card details, address and phone number.

I was so troubled by this risk to her identity, I wrote down the details and texted them to her, explaining the dangers. She got up and walked out of the carriage. I thought I was being helpful!

The one voice I like to be quite loud is a staff member making announcements over the tannoy system; if it is too quiet, I get uneasy. I like regular confirmations that my journey is following the route I am expecting. I get frustrated with other passengers who talk through these announcements and have to stop myself telling them to be quiet. I also love to hear happy people laughing and regaling each other with stories, children in conversation or playing with their families.

One particular problem on a train – being confined to a seat – is the likelihood that passengers may smell particularly strong, whether from personal odours (garlic is a common one) or perfume. I am particularly affected by strong perfumes; indeed, I am sensitive to many which give me headaches, sneezing fits and even itchy eyes and skin. Worse still is when they are actually sprayed on the train, causing the aroma to be even stronger. One tip of mine is to carry around a small spritzer bottle with a fragrance-free facial toner – useful for both autistic overheating moments and also menopausal flushes, if you happen to be of the age and gender! Just be careful not to spray your neighbour; I did this once by accident and she objected very loudly...oops!

If I need to be distracted on a train, and have forgotten to bring a book or music (although rare), I challenge myself to listen for as many sounds as I can. On one short journey I heard:

- creaking sounds from the rails

- emergency vehicle sirens (at station)

- school children shouting
- train announcements
- airplane flying overhead (at station)
- rustling food packets
- pages turning
- keyboards rattling
- alert sounds on digital devices
- coughing and sneezing
- murmuring
- someone talking to herself (oh, actually that was probably me!)
- muffled sounds from music listened to through headphones
- various ring tones on phones including beeps, bells, whistles, a John Wayne movie theme tune and the song from *The Flintstones.*

This can be useful if you have autistic children with you: to actually turn the experience upside down, by purposely listening for sounds as a game, rather than being bothered by them. Otherwise, if they don't have headphones or ear buds to block out the sounds, in addition to the bright lights and strong aromas in the train, they may experience the journey like me, which at times is akin to being trapped in a mobile sensory prison.

I notice that, depending on my sensory status, I can feel particularly hot or cold, despite no change in weather or environment. Even without this overload, I find the range of temperatures on a train vary; one minute I am really hot and the next I am freezing cold. I once sat on a train in a carriage where the heating wasn't working. By the time I reached my destination, I was shivering from head to toe. I walked through another carriage to get off the train and realised that had I walked there sooner, I would not have suffered; it seemed it was just our carriage which was affected. I always dress in layers that can be easily removed, carry a scarf, drink lots of water and make sure my feet are warm.

I relish the times we are going through tunnels; I love this part…it all goes dark and silent; the constant buzzing and beeping and random tunes all stop for just a short while and I can hear myself think once again.

For many years I had a fear of underground trains and stations. I was terrified that I would get lost, get on the wrong train or off at the wrong station. It took a while to get used to but the Underground in London at least is now just a matter of routine for me. I still don't always know exactly where I am going, but I no longer get worried if I make a wrong choice, and I always have a map with me. My anxiety levels do depend on how I am feeling as I enter the station, whether I am in a hurry, whether I am alone or if someone is dependent upon me. In New York City, however, I find the Subway daunting and try to avoid it at all costs, even if it means walking 30 blocks, probably because I don't use the Subway very much and am not used to it. I fear how and when to pay, where to go, where the trains go and how to work out the system. On the one occasion I was bold enough to use the Subway, the train did not stop where I expected it to and I panicked so much that I have never used it again. This, of course, is my perspective and I have no doubt it is just as safe and as easy as the Underground in London. Perhaps I just need to go on it a couple of times with a New Yorker to get to know my way around. Maybe on my next visit?

I have been on the Underground during many rush hours, people scurrying about like a swarm of bees around the honeypot. The noise buzzes in a similar fashion, voices blending together to form a somewhat noisy choir of chatter. Often you will find a busker strumming a sound to make some money or singing for his supper. Some are just trying to gain recognition for a talent unnoticed. In fact, the American music legend Paul Simon began his career in the very same way back in the 1960s. I wonder how much money he made as he sang his wonderful lyrics back then, and whether anyone realised how famous he would become?

When I lived in London, I would travel up and down the Northern Line every day; I still remember the vibrant chatter, the heat as passengers squashed into every crevice of the carriage, and the pungent aromas floating around deep into the summer months – perfume and flowers mixed with sweat, strawberries and last night's curry...a vibrant combination indeed! To cope with the chaos, I generally focused on whatever I was reading at the time. That was back in the 1990s, and mobile phones at that time were brick-sized, mainly used in the car. No e-readers or tablets, just good old-fashioned paper. The aroma of a new book...bliss.

WHEN IT GOES WRONG

The Underground train stopped at a station a few stops from my end destination for an unusually long time and I started to get a niggling butterfly sensation in my belly. After about 15 minutes, an announcement came that the train would not be moving forward and that everyone was to get out and leave the station. This truly was a nightmare for me, especially since it had been a long day and I was feeling somewhat anxious by then.

I was not troubled by the train stopping and having to walk the rest of the way; after all, it was not far and I knew the area really well. For me, the concern was so many people all heading out of the station at once. Of course, it was an inconvenience and there were lots of stressed and angry people rushing around. To make matters worse, there was no escalator at this station, and therefore we all had to wait for just two lifts to street level. People were impatient, as you might imagine. There was pushing and shoving, shouting and loud chatter. Sensory overload was inevitable. I am not sure that my own reactions were the problem for me; after all, I was on my own without having to worry about another person, and I knew where I was and where I needed to go. I know that the calmer I can remain, the easier the situation is for me to deal with. My problem was with the reactions from others. Add this to the additional crowds, and suddenly I felt utterly overwhelmed.

Had my husband been in this situation, he would have become angry at others pushing; with the additional heat, lights and noise, he may have experienced complete meltdown. His perceptions alter when he is put in these situations and he can come across as a tall aggressive man without that being his intention. It is often the case for autistic individuals that we react in surprising and often inappropriate ways – not always predictable. To reiterate, no two autists are alike. We all have our own triggers which affect our behaviour and reactions. This can make life difficult for those around us, and, perhaps surprisingly, for us as well. It is often out of our control.

On a social media newsfeed recently, there was a video of a man at an underground station who began a 'flash mob' song, and eventually everyone standing waiting for the train joined in. I would love for this to happen while I am present. Having researched these flash mob events some more, I now appreciate that they are usually professional singers, actors or dancers who randomly organise such events. That's probably why so many people join in. This revelation leaves me a little disappointed; naively, I thought they were all people like me who had been waiting their whole lives for it to happen to them.

So I shall continue to travel through underground and mainline stations, in the hope that one day I shall be witness to a wonderful flash mob performing a random song or dance. I shall be there among them, giving it my all, probably near the front of the crowd.

I may not be comfortable at random social events where I have talk to people, but I love to dance and perform, given any opportunity.

CHAPTER 5

AQUATICS

This is a particularly short chapter, as I have a strange relationship with water. As a child, I used to swim pretty well and on a regular basis, my dad teaching me at the local pool. Following my illness, I seemed to lose all my confidence and my fear of water began. Even now, my worst fear is to drown, yet I have not had the courage to attempt to swim again bar a few disastrous lessons every now and then.

Water travel is not my favourite mode of transport. On our honeymoon, we paid for an expensive yacht trip and I was asked to leave at the next port, an hour after we left the mainland; I spent the entire hour throwing up. Whether it was nerves or seasickness, I have no idea, but I have not attempted such a journey since.

I can manage a ferry, and just about manage a boat trip across a city waterway, but I will never be someone who loves to sail. Now that I am a practising yogi, my breathing techniques should help me get through a sailing experience, but I admit I am scared to try again.

On a visit to the US state of Florida, many memories stand out for me, including Disney World and Universal Studios. The experience that affected me most, however, was during a short stay in the Florida Keys – the beautiful city of Key West in particular. We decided (well, Joe did really, and I agreed somewhat reluctantly) to try to jet-ski in the incredibly blue waters of the Gulf of Mexico.

He rented a jet ski, we were given a couple of minutes' instruction on how to drive it, and then we were left to it.

Joe drove and I sat behind him, clinging on for dear life. I remember I was wearing sunglasses the whole time as the sun was bright and uncomfortable. He drove slowly at first, to get used to it, and then suddenly he speeded up and I can only describe my feeling as pure fright. I closed my eyes so tightly that I gave myself a headache, and I think I pretty much cried and screamed the whole trip until at last he stopped somewhere in the middle of the ocean. He somehow convinced me to take the controls and drive around for a short amount of time. Surprisingly, I enjoyed this (probably because I was in control), but then I was only driving really slowly. It was a bit like a bumper car but on beautiful clear blue water. The fear began again when Joe took the controls and speeded his way back to the dock. I won't elaborate on the accident we had on the way back, resulting in damage to the jet ski and caused (according to Joe – I had my eyes tightly shut again) by another jet ski coming towards him under a bridge and forcing him to swerve, causing the engine to cut out!

It probably goes without saying at this point that I have never ridden one again since then and definitely never will. Just the experience alone of the water splashing all over my face was enough to cause meltdown, although at the time I thought it was simply the fear of going too fast, rather than the sensory impact of autism.

It is difficult to describe how I feel when water hits my face. It is not the wetness; I use a wrung-out water-soaked cloth to cleanse my face and that's fine. It is the feeling of the splashing I can't cope with, unexpected or not. If someone catches me with a water hose, or I even catch a spray in the dentist's chair, it is as if someone has pricked me all over with sharp knives. I also struggle to plunge my hands into a bowl of cold water; it makes me cringe.

In case you might be wondering, yes, I do wash myself with water. I prefer a shower, and I stand with my back to the shower head, washing my hair with my head back. If I get splashed (this sometimes happens when I am staying in a hotel and I have not used the shower before), you would hear a loud screech from the bathroom. That would be me, trying desperately to grab the towel to wipe it off my face quickly. The last time I had a bath would be years ago; when I was a child, we only had a bath. I always took a book into the bathroom and spent the time reading and swishing a small amount of water and bubble bath around so that it looked as though I had bathed. I just washed in the sink instead. I only confessed this to my mum a couple of years ago. I am told having a bath is a stress reliever – not for me, though!

I have considered venturing on a cruise ship as a form of travel, as they are far larger and there is less chance of splashing, but if I don't like it, I will be trapped for a week or more. Potential anxiety prevents me from trying…for now at least.

EATING OUT

'One cannot think well, love well, sleep well, if one has not dined well.'

Virginia Woolf

CHAPTER 6

FOOD AND DRINK REVEALED

As I write this chapter, I am sipping sharp and spicy lemon and ginger tea from one of my favourite mugs. Experiencing food and drink is very personal and, whether or not you are autistic, you will have a very different perspective to another person.

The eating and drinking experience is multi-sensory. It should not simply be about your enjoying the taste and whether it serves a practical purpose of filling you up, adding nutrients or hydrating you; consumption of food and drink can be so much more of a sensory experience for most people.

I was listening to the radio recently and heard a lady talking about her experience of a car accident which had left her without the senses of smell and taste. She was explaining how she used to love food, but since the accident it was something she consumed simply to live and eating was no longer an enjoyable activity. This made me contemplate my own experiences of gastronomy, feeling grateful for my ability to use all of my senses. Add to this the often heightened senses of an autistic individual, and I feel very fortunate indeed. As I discussed in Chapter 1, some autists can be hyposensitive and therefore may not experience food and drink in the same way as each other.

I have enjoyed walking into a specialist chocolate café, whereupon I was bombarded with beautiful sights and aromas: a glass counter filled with rows and rows of delicate and beautiful sweets and pastries infused with combinations of sweet aromas – vanilla, orange, peppermint, cinnamon, cloves, apple, fennel, liquorice, coconut... As well as the gorgeous aromas, the visual detail was exquisite: pastel icing, flowers, bows and even gold leaf. Visually, the café resembled a gigantic luxury chocolate bar of marble and brick with jewel-coloured chairs, 'marshmallow-like' to add flair and comfort. Faced with such a place, the anticipation of my chosen macaroon and hot chocolixir (a ganache-based hot chocolate drink) filled me with delight, even before they were anywhere near my mouth.

My carefully chosen macaroon was a visual and aromatic spectacle: a tea and almond base filled with a creamy mousse mixture perfumed with 'fragrant Jasmine and Gardenia scent decorated with flower bits of magnolia, cornflower, hibiscus and lavender, served with raspberry coulis' and garnished with gold leaf; each mouthful was a taste sensation, savoured with absolute pleasure. There is a condition that is experienced by few autistic individuals called synaesthesia, where the experience is felt with more than one sense. I can only imagine the rainbow of colours that might be evoked by tasting this divine macaroon. I found a satisfaction in seeking out each individual component ingredient as I ate slowly. Equally, my hot chocolixir was a delicious mix of creamy flavours, topped with sugar 'crystals'. If you are tempted by these delicacies, the café is in a very well-known high-end store in West London, and I believe in a scattering of other cities in the UK.

We may have sharper taste buds than our non-autistic friends and this can be such an advantage when eating out. I love to pick out individual flavours in a dish; I eat more mindfully and savour what I am eating rather than it being simply 'fuel'. I often feel blessed that I am able to experience such intricacies: the subtle pinch of ginger, a touch of lemon, or a wine with a peach undertone.

I wonder how many wine tasters, chocolatiers or perfume experts are autistic but have no idea?

I love to try a variety of food; this is not true for all autistic individuals, however. In fact, one commonality is that autists have a tendency to opt for similar foods and even the same brands of food for much of the time. For anyone with sensory issues, their choices may be influenced by colour, texture, aroma, appearance, taste and even proximity to other foods on the plate. You might have been in a restaurant at one time where there is a screaming child refusing to eat what is on his plate, and thought he was disobedient and badly brought up. In fact, this child might have a sensory disorder, and the beans were touching the sausage, or the minced beef 'tasted' rough – sensory differences his parents might not understand. Of course, he might just be disobedient, but I would like to think we all think twice before we judge without knowing more.

I would always urge you to try something new, providing you are not having an 'autistic day'. It might just be a new vegetable, a different flavour ice cream or a new coffee blend, but you may discover something incredible and be eternally grateful for that one potentially risky move. All your favourite foods were once strangers, but you gave them a chance. My great discovery was avocado which I now love any which way, and my husband would never eat an Indian curry before I introduced him to it when we met. He does still have that same dish 27 years later, but small steps are better than none. That's not to say that at home I don't regularly opt for favourite foods. There is nothing quite like a cheese, tomato and salad cream sandwich for comfort!

One new experience for me was in Copenhagen. The meal was organised by our hosts so I had little choice but to try it. We were given menus from which to choose the foods or, more accurately, the ingredients. We then sat in front of the chef's area to watch as they turned our ingredients into delicious meals. I loved to watch closely as the chef chopped fresh vegetables from big containers or stirred a bubbling pot of stew, and to have the exact foods I wanted freshly prepared was somewhat exciting and therapeutic. The aromas were remarkable and the colours immense as a vast array of ingredients chosen by me and my fellow diners were made quickly into incredible meals. The aroma of freshness was unmistakable, and the fragrances were sensational and plentiful; I was so tempted to delve into the containers and grab handfuls myself to just smell them close up.

Had someone given me the choice before going to this restaurant, I probably would have said no, as I would have been anxious about what to expect. I am so glad I had no choice. In Helsinki, I was given a meal including reindeer meat. Again, I would usually have not chosen this, but it was pleasant enough, although I found the texture a little odd.

Often I can't eat a foodstuff not because of the taste but because of the texture. One that springs to mind is the pear. The taste is exquisite, but I cannot bear the grainy texture and so I avoid eating pears. Texture can be so personal, and for an autistic individual this can be the make-or-break factor for many foods. Generally, I love panettone, the Italian spongy cake, often eaten (by me at least) at Christmas. I actually love the little bits of citrus peel the most. However, one time I was in a restaurant and chose panettone for dessert. It was a more unusual chocolate pudding, delicious in flavour (after all, it was chocolate), but I can only describe the texture as thick, stodgy, doughy and frankly disgusting.

Some foods are all about the texture, though, and I love them just for this reason – potato crisps, for example, which have that satisfying crunch, or a ripe fig dripping with juice. We autists love particular textures and the feel of them in our mouths; as a child, I devoured anything icy. When no one was looking, I would scrape ice from around the edge of the freezer box and eat it out of a cup. I am always tempted to lick snow just to feel that texture on my tongue once more in the face of the more modern self-defrosting freezers. Apparently, my husband was partial to the texture of coal on his tongue as a child…hmmm.

Actually, there is often an autistic need to taste something just to find out what the texture is, and this is not always food (as proved by Joe's coal); fabrics such as velvet and chenille are favourites of mine, and I once licked a stair hand rail in a restaurant as it was smooth and cold and I was desperate to find out how it felt on my tongue. This may sound odd to you, but I am sure there are a few of you reading this, nodding your head and thinking, 'I am not alone, then.' The autistic person will think or feel it and actually do it; the non-autistic person may think it, but would never actually do it. Stepping out of our comfort zone may have benefits which override the potential discomfort or embarrassment. It is not, in my opinion, wrong, but not considered the 'norm' by most people. I digress…but for good reason here, I believe.

The multi-sensory nature of food means that we perceive flavour with our eyes and our noses as well as with our tongues. Aromas create anticipation. How often have you watched food brought to the table, and you start to salivate with the anticipation of what it will taste like? Pasta, gleaming with olive oil; hot baked potatoes dripping with butter; steaming fresh vegetables in a rainbow of colours; goat's cheese and figs, drizzled with honey; a large beaker of steaming hot chocolate; or a glass of Merlot, rich with blackcurrant, vanilla and oak.

I also have a slight addiction (is this an oxymoron?) to pea shoots, which seem to be a favourite of chefs in modern cuisine. I even pick them as I walk around gardens where vegetables are growing.

There are times, however, when anticipation will turn into disappointment; the food or drink will not live up to your expectations. I often take lots of time to choose my food when I am dining out; there is that choice between a dish I have had before and know I love and trying something new. Often I will have the choice in my head, and when I am finally asked to place my order, I will change my mind at the last minute out of sheer panic. These changes have a way of disappointing me and mostly I regret that change of mind. Perhaps, instead of choosing that chocolate panettone, I should have stuck to my usual dessert choice of cheesecake! I am also partial to crème brûlée; it's the crunch of the topping which is satisfying both visually and audibly, as well as the delicious custard underneath.

Although food in the usual restaurants, cafés and tea shops is wonderful, for me there is a certain excitement in food prepared on the spot from a street vendor. Wandering among the stalls in certain areas of cities, where the variety is in abundance, is an incredible experience. Choices of local and international foods sit side by side: curries, noodles, falafels, pizza, burgers, jerk chicken, paella, kebabs, burritos and fish and chips, together with cinnamon doughnuts, Mexican churros, pretzels and sugared peanuts. Eating from street vendors takes away the uncertainty of walking into a store and not knowing whether to sit down or order at the counter; I can smell the food immediately and make an informed choice. I can usually see the vendor cooking the food and therefore know that the 'kitchen' is clean...or not.

I also adore festive markets which are full of delicious aromas wafting from little wooden chalet-style huts. Rarer delicacies such as buffalo or kangaroo burgers and bratwurst are sold alongside rows of olives, pungent cheeses, syrupy crêpes, mulled wine and gingerbread hot chocolate. What's not to love? I never know quite where to eat, though: while walking, find a bench or – my temptation – sit in the middle of the street and enjoy the food without worrying (I never do, of course, as it is apparently not appropriate, especially as an adult).

Foods being sold in markets or on the streets could be a delight to any autistic individual. The variety of colours, aromas and textures are in abundance, the food is instant and needs no waiting, and often one can sample what is on offer. Whether it is a meal or simply a bag of nuts, the sensory experience is immediate. For some of you with a need to stay away from crowds and the possibility of being touched or bumped into, there may be more planning needed to choose a market carefully. But for others, the outdoor 'see and buy' experience should fulfil food wishes. It is worth remembering that some autistic individuals, however, may find these collective food areas too stimulating for their senses and even overwhelming. I love them, though, and try to follow my nose to the aromas that attract me the most and hope that the taste and textures will live up to the expectation. If not, I have tried something new and learned a lesson never to try it again.

And who doesn't like an ice lolly or swirly cone-type ice cream from a street vendor? Childhood memories are wrapped up in licking around and around until my tongue has to squeeze inside the cone to empty it completely; am I the only one to throw the cone away once the ice cream is gone, though? It's a texture thing...

CHAPTER 7

I LOVE A PLATE

People in the food industry haven't always made eating out easy for us in recent years. Not only do we have to choose where or what we eat, based on location, food type, environment and ambience, lighting or how busy it is; now we also have to consider how the food is served and whether that satisfies our senses or creates havoc with them. Here, I mean to consider on what the food is served.

I dined out with a group of acquaintances a couple of years ago at a restaurant where they served lots of small dishes of food, tapas style, for the table to share. One person, a regular customer, ordered the food, as she apparently knew what was good. What I didn't expect was that most of the food would be served on a variety of objects other than china. Meat was on wooden boards, bread was in a cage, butter in marble dishes and so on. The butter made sense as marble presumably keeps it cold, and at least it was a hard, smooth dish. The rest, though, was not for me; I was limited to just a few dishes I could, or would, eat.

This trend has been growing for a few years now; there has even been a social media campaign to highlight the idiocy of the practice, which apparently is to make the restaurant stand out among the rest.

My number one objection is the lack of hygiene; how does one properly clean a wooden board with knife marks on it, where blood has been seeping from a rare steak, for example? At home, I don't use wooden chopping boards or wooden spoons for this reason; wood is a porous substance, after all. One of my anxieties is that the wood may splinter and be left in my food. The same can be said for slate, which surely chips easily; I know that my kitchen floor does. Some would say that it is about being at one with nature, and therefore a healthy option. I get splinters in the garden from wooden fences. That doesn't mean I want to eat egg and chips on a fence panel! Nor do I want my gravy spilling over the edge of a piece of slate.

It might be shocking but the photo above shows sausage, beans and chips served in a dog bowl, in a real eatery. My dogs would love to be served this, but I would rather miss this meal entirely. Imagine the horror for autistic individuals who hate their foods touching each other.

Other serving 'plates' I have been offered throughout a variety of cities, and not just in the larger ones, include roof tiles, buckets, flower pots, shoes and shells. This trend also extends to drinks, with jam jars being a popular vessel of choice in some bars and cafés.

I am convinced that serving food on wood and other materials essentially changes the taste and smell of the food. This change can be acute for autistic individuals; remembering that we are usually hyper- or hyposensitive, even the smallest difference can be noticed. There is also an added danger that an autist may prefer the alternative to the food itself. A coal dish of ice cream, anyone?

With the popularity of this practice, I now have a tendency to ring ahead to ask what food is served on, especially in gastropubs or more trendy restaurants. I no longer eat meat, but this makes me especially aware if I am brought, for example, a sandwich or veggie burger on a slab of wood. Has this same slab been used for a steak previously? How do they know which ones have been used for what?

If I am brought any food on wood or any other alternative to china, I will always send it back and ask for it to be transferred to a plate. I was once told they didn't have plates big enough for my pizza, so I told them to cut it up and pile it on to the plate instead. My only concession is when fries are brought out in a little metal bucket (usually also wrapped in greaseproof paper or a paper doily). I actually quite like them sitting vertically as they are easier to pick up and eat, in my opinion.

Even when china is used, restaurants often try to be different and risk practicality for presentation. While I love a plate, not all plates are created equal. Recently I was served food in a dish-type plate, with a small space in the middle and a rim which was three or four inches across. The food needed to be cut up, which was a problem. The hole was not big enough to use, and the rim was not stable enough. Every time I tried to cut, the 'dish' fell sideward. I gave up in frustration and couldn't finish the meal.

Enough now with the style over content. I am the first one to delight in a visually pleasing meal, but if I struggle to eat it, or it tastes strange because it is served on a chunk of tree, it takes the pleasure out of the experience. The flavour then becomes a secondary consideration.

Let's stick to rustic furniture, please, if you love wood so much, and let the food remain the star of the meal!

CHAPTER 8

WHERE AND WHEN

There are times when I simply want to eat my meal and leave; indeed, I see many people shovel down their food, not allowing time to taste the flavours, to appreciate the time the chef has spent preparing the dish, or even to chew the food. The result will usually be an over-full belly, indigestion and a bill for the privilege. This is rare for me, though. I think eating out should be about so much more.

I especially find that having more time to eat and to relax while doing so sets up my day or evening well while I am outside the home, preventing a build-up of negative events that will potentially cause sensory meltdown. Being in the right environment can be so rewarding, even inspiring; I love to be inspired, as a writer and as a sentient being. In between courses, or even mouthfuls, I think, write, read or dream of new ventures, movies to watch or books to write, as I did with this one: I was having a delicious brunch in a favourite brasserie, while listening to the sounds of Sinatra and sipping a latte. I also love to listen and really hear. Our hyper-acute senses can often catch even the slightest noise. When a restaurant is full of customers, the combined chatter can just be a blur of noise for most, but for autists, conversations across the room can often be heard clearly; I liken this to a radio being tuned. Once tuned into a specific distant conversation, we can often hear every nuance. A restaurant with fewer customers mainly yields staff pottering around, providing an opportunity to really open the senses and hear everything around. Life is to be enjoyed, and when I listen, I hear staff going about their work quietly singing or chattering with each other as they set up tables and fill bar shelves with clattering crockery or cutlery.

By listening carefully to what is going on in an environment, there is the opportunity to use imagination and creativity – ideals that, apparently, we autists are not supposed to have. I disagree, however; as a telephone rings, I imagine the person at the other end excitedly booking a table for a special occasion or simply to meet a friend. Who knew the brewing of coffee could excite so many senses if you just open them up to it? I hear chug-chugs and whooshes as the dark liquid gold bubbles with its nearly burnt aroma. Just breathing this aroma in awakens me and gives me the feeling I am tasting its rich pungency.

Do you too find it fascinating how the senses work? Just one song or aroma can take us back to a moment in time. I marvel at the power the senses have within us, and for autistic individuals this power may be magnified several times over. Music choice in a restaurant is key to a comfortable experience; the wrong type, or music that is too loud, can ruin the experience, more so for an autistic individual. We often find it problematic to distinguish between background and foreground noise, and loud music distorts the gap between the two, making it impossible to hear the important information and to zone out the irrelevant sounds. My husband can hear conversations going on across a room but not always hear what I am saying to him while I sit across the table. This is not (usually) selective hearing, but a genuine difficulty in filtering sounds. Not only can this be annoying and frustrating, but it can cause physical pain in the head and eyes with the sheer effort of trying to separate sounds.

A meal out can be so exhausting for this reason alone. If you are dining alone and have this difficulty in filtering sounds, you might want to carry headphones or ear buds with you. If it all gets too much, you have a way to shut everyone out of your head while you enjoy your food. I do this only occasionally, as I feel safer if I can hear what is going on, but it is something my husband does regularly when he is getting anxious in busy restaurants.

It can be difficult for autistic individuals to soothe their thoughts and just be. I am getting much better at doing this, as I practise meditation which has helped enormously. My imagination still runs riot, though, and I would hate to lose this even though it can be terribly exhausting. If I am seated near a window, I cannot help but watch and wonder: for example, about the dust trucks collecting bin bags full of items people consider no longer relevant or important to their lives; empty burger cartons, coffee cups, and enough food waste to feed the millions of hungry people around the world who would cherish such delights.

My mind is always whirring, throwing out information that may be important but often has to be simply discarded. I try to quieten my mind, but it can be like a conveyor belt, going around and around on a loop, repeating itself endlessly. Autists' perception is often very acute, and we notice small details which might be missed by the non-autistic person. Many autists love to count items, often subconsciously; lights, railings, chairs, tiles, pictures on walls are all items to be counted, but I wonder if you, like me, get frustrated when you see dead lightbulbs, unlit candles and wonky pictures. My focus is usually on the symmetry; tables and chairs are ideally in absolutely straight lines which look as though they have been measured to perfection. If I walk past them, I like to touch them, to satisfy my visual perception as correct.

Individuals have their own focus and see things differently, which makes the world a fascinating place to be; an autist's perception tends to be very different and often bizarre to the average person. Our thoughts make absolute sense – or they do to us at least – and our thoughts and words are usually simple, obvious or literal. I love places where everything is clean, shiny, comfortable and homely (in Denmark they call this Hygge). I appreciate when the temperature is just right; for an autistic person, temperature extremes can be unbearable, causing other sensory differences to surface, as I shall explain later.

The eating-out experience in the city, of course, starts with where to go. For some, this is an easy decision, often based on food type, location or recommendation. For autistic individuals, there are many other factors to consider. Not only might eating out involve social gatherings – difficult enough for us – but it also comprises many sensory triggers; we have to choose our eatery carefully. There are many variables which have a great impact on our experience, but for this chapter I shall concentrate on where and when.

An autistic friend cannot eat in a restaurant at night where the lights are full on; it is simply too much for her to bear, especially combined with the buzzing chatter from other customers and the usual restaurant sounds, so appreciated by me when a restaurant is near to empty. She is likely to suffer headaches, pain behind her eyes, and her sense of taste is altered so that the food texture and taste become repugnant. When her senses are overloading, she rocks urgently in a bid to calm herself down. Continued overload can result in a rage ensuing without any apparent warning either to her or to anyone around her. I can usually see the signs, but unless I can remove her from the situation easily, this is not always helpful. Once overload is present, she has the strength of

Popeye eating spinach, and everything and everyone in her path will go flying.

Personally, I can cope with the brighter lights, providing it is the only sensory trigger and I am not already anxious. Open-plan restaurants where you can watch the chefs in the kitchen, for example, may cause sensory overload in some autistic individuals. There are more noises, more aromas, more of everything. I love to smell the heady mix from the kitchen – for me, it adds to the atmosphere – but there are limitations. A favourite vegan café of mine is a place of joy for breakfast or from mid-afternoon onwards, but it is not for me at lunchtimes. Not only is it quite small and therefore 'claustrophobic' when busy and noisy, but the open-plan kitchen often exudes steamy, cloudy and choking smells which sting the eyes and irritate the throat. Normally, I would recommend open-plan restaurants as they can soak up the noise from customers, but not necessarily in a smaller establishment.

I do love to see the chef cooking, though; it gives me great confidence in the food if I can see the processes and nothing is hidden away. One restaurant in central London is such a place, where there are always wonderful aromas wafting from the hot plates of chili, fennel, garlic and basil. The food is incredible, despite some dishes usually being served on slabs of wood (horror!); it is worth asking for a china plate here just to experience the amazing food.

There are eateries where the lights are dimmed, or candles are used as the room gets busier and consequently louder; this creates a much warmer feeling and takes away the harsh bright lights. Staff recognise the sensory overload of customers and compensate for it by changing the ambience. For individuals with a propensity to sensory overload, this compensatory measure is very welcome, especially as the evening gets darker.

If I am feeling relaxed and am not in a hurry, I try to push myself to try unfamiliar eateries. I tend to choose these based on how friendly they look from the outside, but only if there is a menu in the window so that I am satisfied I will like the food choices. Quiet and calm atmosphere, comfortable furniture and temperature, delicious food – an autistic individual would be happy with these variables. Sometimes all we need is to appreciate what is around us; my courage is often rewarded and yours could be too. If it does not work out well, at you least you will have tried something new. I found a fantastic place for breakfast in London – full of enormous silver pipes running around the room, nicely juxtaposed with a large crystal chandelier which made for an attention-grabbing sight. I find variations in textures exciting and I loved this contradiction of objects. The overriding aroma was of freshly sawn timber – a personal favourite: walls were covered with rough-sawn wood and there was sawdust on the floor, much like an American style bar in the movies. These features gave the place a wonderful relaxed, informal and quirky character, and the staff were similarly calm, relaxed and friendly. The blueberry and buttermilk pancakes were a delicious bonus that made my taste buds tingle with happiness. This type of experience makes trying somewhere new worthwhile, and I would urge you to try for yourself when you are having a calm day.

That's not to say I feel able to venture into new places all the time, and when I do, I am not always calm. There are always initial anxieties of whether I will feel comfortable, what I should do, will I enjoy the food? Despite enjoying new sensory stimulation, there is often a fine line between enjoying a multitude of sensory experiences and experiencing sensory overload, and the tumble across the line can be quick and unrelenting.

At times, it can make me want to shout and scream, or even sob out loud to take away the overwhelming feelings of discomfort and pain.

Like a child, I am drawn to shiny, bright things, but often when I engage, the experience turns into a sensory nightmare. One such encounter with a restaurant yielded this effect. The dining area was visually amazing, set against an ultraviolet-blue backlit wall, and contained tables under-lit with a bright white light. I was drawn in as soon as I spotted it; I instantly wanted to touch everything.

When my food arrived, I realised that the combination of the blue and the bright white-lit tables was a big mistake for someone who experiences sensory differences, and I started to panic. Because the lights were coming from under the table, everything on top was dark. I like to see the food I am eating, and with this light I could barely see any detail of what I was putting into my mouth. As someone who has a tendency to scrutinise every aspect of her food before starting to eat, I found this extremely disconcerting. I was so affected that I nearly got up and left immediately without eating anything, but embarrassment stopped me. I managed to calm myself enough to eat a forkful of avocado (I think), and then my mouth blew up...or so it seemed. They had put some kind of hot dressing on (apparently, it was called chipotle) – and spicy didn't even cover it. A lovely avocado and chicken salad ruined. Note to self: in future, always ask for dressings on the side rather than mixed into the food. Of course, because I couldn't see the food, I couldn't even avoid the particularly sauce-covered parts.

I will admit to you now, the waiter had told me the food was spicy – me being my 'normal' self, I had assumed it would be fine. Lesson learned; if they say it is spicy, it's a warning: IT IS. Don't choose it; there is no shame in saying no. Embarrassment often stops me getting what

I want. Why?! Why do I feel embarrassed asking for what I want or sending it back if I make a wrong choice? This restaurant was beautiful in a bright kind of way. To eat in – never again! I am proud of myself that I even attempted it, but I wish I had chosen somewhere else. Each experience, positive or not, is just that – an experience. It either tells you to repeat it or to learn a lesson from it. Unfortunately for autists, the bad experience can last in our minds for an incredibly long time.

I can generally eat in most places, but for me the 'when' is the crucial element to consider. I have experimented over the years to find eating situations I am comfortable with. I find that three o'clock in the afternoon tends to be a quiet time in restaurants and cafés and can be useful for a late lunch or early dinner, providing it doesn't trigger physical problems such as low blood sugar levels, dizziness or headaches. Similarly, late morning is my favourite time for the ever-popular brunch, a meal with connotations of being laid-back and relaxed – surely a revered notion for us autistic souls.

Eating out in the evening can be more challenging, and my husband and I have always avoided most restaurants at weekends unless we are away from home and do not have a choice. Otherwise, I would suggest choosing an evening during the week when it is usually much quieter; Mondays tend to be our favourite night, or an earlier time slot before the busy period. There will be not only less noise, but often faster service (I can be very impatient and grouchy when I am hungry) and more choice of where to sit. We also choose evening restaurants based on lighting. Candlelight or dimmed wall lighting create a relaxed ambience, and candles focus the eyes and calm anxieties, a technique used in meditation to relax or energise the mind.

Familiarity is important to autistic individuals, especially in times of anxiety. When I want to feel comforted, to get a leisurely drink or pastry without being anxious, to sit and read or write in a relaxed manner, I always head for a familiar coffee shop, one that is pretty much the same in every city, where I know what to order without looking at the menu and know what it will taste like. There are many in cities throughout the world and, like me, you probably have your favourite. I originally chose mine because of the calm colour scheme and the sensory memories this stirs; a vanilla and deep-red décor with lots of dark wood evokes memories of the tubs of ice cream my dad bought for me as a young child – a smooth, creamy swirl of chocolate, vanilla and strawberry. Just scrumptious. The coffee shop similarly yields aromas of sweet vanilla and spices from the amazing cakes and pastries, mixed with the unmistakable smell of rich coffee.

Some of you may not like to visit these coffee shops as they can get busy, and there are so many often-confusing choices to make just for a hot drink: small, regular, grande, tall, venti, short, full-fat, skinny, soy, coconut, syrup shots, decaf, iced, extra hot (some autistic individuals who have hypotactile sensitivities have a high pain threshold so this choice is useful) and so on. My advice: find your favourites through trial and error and then stick to them, even when they introduce specials. Black forest gateau hot chocolate, anyone? Yuk!

My only grumble is that when I walk in, there are tables free, and by the time I go to sit down, they can be taken by people standing behind me who have either put their bags on seats in advance or have a friend or children who can grab a table. This causes me undue anxiety and frustration. Although I now try to venture into new and independent places more often, I still head for the familiar when I feel the need, rather like eating comfort food when it is cold outside or you feel sad or upset.

I am also constantly on the lookout in cities for kitchen- or den-style coffee or tea shops, with squishy sofas, armchairs and low-level tables offering a range of simple healthy, organic foods and beverages detailed on large blackboards. These are gradually becoming 'my familiar'. I feel very 'chilled out' and unperturbed in these places, and I am encouraged to stay longer than I would normally – especially a favourite of mine in New York City where staff wander around with large pots of coffee, filling up mugs as they chat to customers. It is a place of refuge and community in an otherwise gargantuan city (one that I love). For autists with sensory overload, this kind of place might be ideal: lovely textures, simple décor, soft music and simple enjoyable food all wrapped up in a calm environment. Some autistic individuals who have difficulties with adjusting their bodies to different positions (proprioception) might also find it easier to relax or work with less formal seating and a quieter buzz of happy but relaxed customers.

I have been travelling away from home for many years, working and studying, and I have found various places of comfort and tranquillity within cities I visit; hotel restaurants and lounge bars tend to be my quiet places in cities, where I go to get peace and to calm any sensory overload. As a result, I am inclined towards comfortable and simple surroundings with some interest. These may, of course, depend on the hotel, the time of day and even the city, but you will likely have your favourites; if not, it may be time to check some out in the cities you visit regularly.

My only gripe in many hotel dining rooms would have to be the temperature. Autistic individuals often have differences in thermoception to individuals not on the spectrum; we have an altered sense of temperature in our body. Extremes of hot and cold may feel particularly uncomfortable, but not only that, they affect how our other senses work as well. If I am particularly cold, I find my hearing gets worse, I feel extreme physical pain, and my sense of touch and taste are affected. I always wear lots of layers and a scarf to cover all eventualities, and especially in case the temperature dips or the air conditioning is on full strength; even in the summer, air conditioning can be brutal. Cold can also affect my visual perception and getting up to walk to the toilet, for example, might be difficult as my balance may be affected – even without a couple of glasses of wine! Perhaps they should follow the example of one restaurant I visited where each table had a button which controlled a personal heater around the table, allowing heat to be switched on or off at the will of the customer. Now that was a fabulous idea for customer comfort.

Some hotel restaurants I love for the visual interest, and one such favourite is shown in the photo on the previous page. There is an interesting divider between the formal and informal zones of the dining area which I spend time staring at and touching the symmetrical rows of identical bottles and the crisscross pattern of the Perspex. You may have the same urge as me to touch objects which appear to be visually interesting. This is common for autists; I find tactile objects very exciting, and they influence so much in my life: what I buy, where I go, my choices and my preferences.

Sounds also play a big part in an autistic individual's sensory experience. My husband is more sensitive to background noise than I am; I can happily sit in a coffee house or restaurant and enjoy listening to what is going on around me, as long as I am not feeling overloaded for any prior reason. He would much rather head towards a quiet hotel. He says it is a peaceful haven among the bustle of the city. He too has his favourites, based on quietness, free Wi-Fi availability, the food and the fabric of the chairs and cushions (in that order); he finds many textures supremely uncomfortable even through his clothes, and can find many chairs cause him physical pain on his skin. Just a minor irritation can cause his skin to turn red, itchy and painful.

Whichever city he happens to be in, if he can find a quiet hotel to eat in, he will always choose this option. Crowded rooms always bring out stimming in him; for him, this consists of leg rubbing (in circles) or virtual writing at speed on the table (he will usually write words that are whizzing around in his head). These repetitive movements calm him to some degree and give him something else to focus on when external sensory stimulants are becoming too much for him.

Sometimes it is worth staying within your comfort zone; only you can decide, but how calm your day has been will usually determine how far you are prepared to step out and be daring.

Wherever I am, when I am alone especially, I am quite finicky about where I sit. I like to sit with my back to the wall, preferably on bench-type seats. I feel safer here as no one can come up behind me (martial arts training and my husband constantly reminding me about safety), and I can see what everyone else is doing, which takes away the element of surprise. In my experience, autistic individuals prefer to know what is going on or spend considerable time planning to ensure surprises or shocks will be minimal. Additionally, sitting in such a position makes my body feel grounded, which is comforting; autists often feel vulnerable if they do not know exactly where their body is situated. This grounding is a concept that is important in yoga as well, as a way of connecting physically and psychologically to the earth. For autists, this connectivity makes us feel safer and part of the wider community, rather than being isolated by our autism and our sensory differences. I would never choose a seat in the centre of a restaurant unless there was some kind of divider to protect my back. I also like to sit higher if possible; some places have raised seating, alcoves or cubicles, higher tables and chairs or variations of these. It just feels safer somehow and reduces the intense feeling of vulnerability. I also like that I can see more of what is going on around the room.

If I cannot sit with my back to the wall, I prefer to sit around the edge of the room, by a window if possible. I certainly feel less vulnerable, but also I lose my sense of direction quite easily in unfamiliar places, and the edge is easier to find again if I go to the loo, for instance. I have lost my way back to the table before, when I have had to find a table in among lots of others, and then panic sets in and I tend to bump into people and furniture as my coordination can be affected. With panic comes disarray of many senses at once.

I rarely make choices on where I eat simply based on being autistic; I try not to let it rule my life, although it is always a part of me. Sometimes I have experiences that are unpleasant, and I am not entirely sure whether autism has a part to play or whether they are just very bad experiences. For example, we do not deal well with disappointment or change in expectations. If we experience a negative sensory stimulant, or a build-up of these, the combination can cause anxiety, aggression or withdrawal. You may at times, like me, just want to 'disappear' when things have become too much. Depending on the circumstances, I can become very quiet and withdrawn, or loud and argumentative, even though I do not feel comfortable doing so. It is usually out of my control, and it takes a lot of my energy to stop myself running from the room screaming loudly.

As an autistic adult, I have trained myself over the years to stay composed in public and get myself away from a situation as quickly as possible to calm down privately. Sadly, this ability to appear 'normal' can be detrimental to us, in that we are not always believed when we say we have difficulties in various situations and we are often thought to be making a big fuss over nothing. For people who consider that autism can be mild (I am diagnosed with Asperger's Syndrome, so I get assumptions like this often), believe me: wherever a person is on the spectrum, it can often be considerably more than mild. It just looks mild or even non-existent to an outsider – a passer-by who has never ventured into an autistic head.

I try not to worry about what other people think about my situation; I just continue to do what is best for me. If that involves eating somewhere that has chairs, cushions or tablecloths made out of tactile fabrics such as velvet and brocade, or bumpy seersucker fabric which feels like bubble wrap to stroke, then I will be in sensory heaven and forget about all that is negative around me.

CHAPTER 9

PEOPLE MAKE A DIFFERENCE

Autistic individuals are all very different; for some, eating out might be absolutely fine, whereas for others there will be a whole host of stressors, most of which I have discussed in previous chapters.

For me, the experience is usually dependent on other people: the person or people I am dining with, who else might be in the restaurant or café, and even the staff to some degree.

If the person I am with is someone I am close to – a friend or family member – then the experience will usually go well enough. I have already discussed that dinner with my husband may be difficult in noisy eateries, where it can be difficult to hear each other, and other stressors may affect our sensory and eating experience – bright lights for one. Any bad eating experience we have had is usually because of other people: people on the next table speaking or laughing loudly, a baby screaming as he waits to be fed, a child running around a restaurant noisily without adult supervision.

There is always a danger in restaurants of large parties of people coming in or the noise levels increasing quickly. This can alter the meal experience in seconds, and I try to avoid popular 'party venues' – usually those where they can easily set up large tables, or where food is relatively inexpensive and has a huge variety. For this reason, in cities you might visit often, I would suggest knowledge of quiet places to go to as well as noise-cancelling headphones for emergency use. Of course, if you are with someone else, this is more difficult to resolve and the only option may be to leave. I have been known to use speedy meditation exercises or repeat a short mantra, both of which can be done pretty much anywhere and can quickly calm anxieties. Stepping into the unknown is relatively safe as long as you have a backup plan.

Many autistic individuals do not like to eat with unfamiliar people. I will confess business dining is not an activity I enjoy, probably due to social reasons more than sensory, but autistic all the same. I find that I can get very anxious, and it is the increased anxiety which causes sensory challenges; the more anxious I get, the hotter I become, for example, and body temperature extremes are very common in autists, as you now know. With a high body temperature, eating a hot meal then becomes so uncomfortable that other quirks – for example, rocking or swaying – may become noticeable. With this then comes embarrassment and the whole situation can quickly become out of hand, potentially causing a meltdown with tears or an angry outburst.

Some time ago, this happened to my husband while we were seated at a dining table with people we did not know at a charity function. A conversation was making him uncomfortable to the point that his face became very red and his anxieties were clearly about to 'burst out loud'. Luckily, someone interrupted the conversation, giving us the opportunity to leave the room quickly while he slowly calmed down. These kinds of situations can be so extreme for us that they can cause loss of balance, loss of hearing or zone-out (where the person completely shuts down and blanks out everything around him), dizziness and nausea.

We find ourselves going back time and time again to restaurants where we have become accustomed to the staff, and they in turn know our quirks and preferences.

It might be our preference for sitting at the round table in the corner away from the main restaurant (this one is true for at least three places we visit), or that we like particular drinks pre-meal, or that we prefer the candle on the table to be lit and the main lights dimmed. Staff can make an experience; it is another form of comfort blanket to visit a place where you are made to feel at home. I digress, but this reminds me of the 1980s American comedy show *Cheers* 'where everybody knows your name, and they're always glad you came'!

I know of autistic people who simply hate to eat out in a public place, regardless of the environment or people around them. They would prefer to eat sandwiches in hotel rooms, or eat at home with the family rather than subject themselves to the 'dining out' experience. I have found a solution for this fear while away from home in some cities, which I shall discuss in the next chapter.

I make no apologies for repeating constantly: we are all different and we need to make a choice based on our own experiences and the comfort zones we are willing to live within or step outside of.

CITY LIVING

'Nature does not hurry, yet everything is accomplished.'

Lao Tzu

CHAPTER 10

HOME FROM HOME

Living in the city is both exhilarating and exhausting: a juxtaposition of extremes. One of the most important decisions to be made when 'living' away from home in a city is where to 'live' – that is, where should I stay which will make my experience comfortable and enjoyable; somewhere I can go back to when everything around me becomes too much; where I can, if I so wish, connect to my real home and my family and friends? The decision is important for autistic individuals especially, be it for just one night, or several days or weeks.

My first instinct is not to choose where I stay based on my sensory needs, but based on how close it is to (a) the railway station or large car park, and (b) the venue of the event for which I am visiting the city, or the city centre if I am there simply to shop or sightsee. Do I stay in a hotel or bed and breakfast (guest house), or do I rent an apartment?

Planning a trip to a city which involves an overnight stay is, for me and many other autistic individuals, akin to researching an extensive article I might write in a magazine. It involves many hours of sitting in front of a computer, checking out possible accommodation and even areas around it, including the street views so that I know exactly what it looks like and what neighbouring facilities are available. It can be a fine balance of location versus amenities. Once I have found an ideal location, I proceed to check out every photo available online so that I can choose a room based on comfort, decoration, bathroom facilities and where the rooms are in relation to the bar, restaurant, food or ice vending machines and any function rooms. Knowing about these things gives me at least some control over my stay and prevents disappointment when I arrive.

I was situated above a function room on one stay, only to be kept up until 2am with a party on the floor below, and then further woken as guests went from room to room, giggling and shouting, to continue their fun privately. The music was so loud that the floor vibrated, which was most disconcerting. The next day, I had back-to-back lectures, and the lack of sleep exacerbated my autistic differences very negatively. Any little incident seemed enormous, and a collection of these could have led to meltdown quite quickly. As an example, for autistic individuals, dropping a toothpaste tube lid down the plughole could be on a par with burning your neck with a straightening iron as far as stress levels go. A culmination of these small events could easily be disastrous and deeply distressing; it would be an 'autistic day'. I would now always recommend asking for a room away from any communal areas.

Each type of accommodation has its own pros and cons; for autistic individuals, many additional needs should be taken into account. If you are a regular visitor to a city, I would always try to stay in the same place each time, especially if the visit is for work or training. There will likely be enough anxiety surrounding the reason for the visit, without the accommodation causing more. If the visit is for a less formal reason – visiting the theatre, a family lunch, or to shop, for example – I may be inclined to be just a little more flexible on where I stay.

For example, when I was visiting a particular city every couple of months for over four years to study, I always stayed at the same hotel. As I walked into the foyer, it felt like being back at my second 'home'. Most staff members were familiar, I knew where everything was, and I even had the same room each time. Familiarity when I am away is always comforting; staff learned about my particular quirks and needs. I was told, for example, if a large party was taking place, and I would then eat earlier or eat in my room.

They would seat me at a quiet breakfast table where headphones and a television were available, so that I did not have to engage with other diners as far as possible. Engaging socially with strangers is not easy for me as I am not very good at, or interested in, small talk, so to do this first thing in the morning is an unrivalled effort. Even at home, breakfast is a time I like to be silent. I need routine in the morning to start a good day, so any interruption or change to this might affect the way I feel and react throughout the rest of the day. In hotels, breakfast time always seems to be the busiest and noisiest and I can find it quite testing in several ways:

- Background noises, including chatting and dishes clanging, always seem louder in the morning.

- If I am alone, I feel that everyone is staring at me.

- People are rushing around the restaurant rather than being seated as they are at most other meals.

- Having to keep getting up and down to fetch things can often result in my banging into tables and people in my hurry to sit back down. I can become quite uncoordinated when I get anxious.

We had a long trip one time, where we drove around Florida, staying in various cities and various different hotels and guest houses. I found it most stressful; I had no guarantee of where we would stay, no home from home to comfort me. To survive this trip, I sought out the familiar along the way: we ate in several Chinese restaurants as I love all Chinese food; we played relaxing music while driving; I devoured the local map (we had no satellite navigation) to convince myself we were in the right place. Some autistic individuals may love this kind of trip, but it was not for me – an adventure step too far.

Wherever I stay, I just love the first walk into the room, when I have battled with the 'credit card' key and won, and I am entering my new safe place for at least one night.

I spend time just taking in my surroundings, which creates positive sensory feelings: the crisp bed linen, the statement artwork, the blackout curtains and the various lamps around the room. I spend a few minutes switching the lighting on and off to find which light best suits my eyes. Very busy patterns – wallpapers, bed linen and carpets – can make me feel dizzy or give me motion sickness – hence my research on room decoration before booking. It may sound odd to some of you, but I also spend some time walking around the room – literally around the walls – taking in the shape of the room and where the main objects are within it. This helps me to focus on what I might bump into, especially if I am in a hurry to leave or I visit the loo during the night. It establishes, in my head, the boundaries of my space.

One hotel I stayed in took this to a whole other level. It had in it a double bed, a small desk and a small open wardrobe. The rest of the wall space was taken up with the door to the equally small shower room. I found myself hitting my head on the wall during the night as I leaned forward or moved around. It also felt extremely claustrophobic. At least I couldn't get lost in this room; my boundaries were evident!

There are also specific checks I have to make as an autistic individual to establish that I can use all of the items provided: the sheets, for instance, have to be smooth and on top of a mattress cover; I won't use the towels unless they are soft (if they are scratchy, I will call housekeeping for new ones); and mugs or cups have to be crack- and chip-free if I am to use them for making tea or coffee. A crack or chip would render the receptacle unsanitary, and just seeing one on a plate, for example, would make me send back a whole meal rather than take any risk, however minor. My husband would also add here that if the cushions are rough or scratchy in any way, they have to be kept off the bed and put out of sight in the wardrobe if possible. Autistic individuals experience roughness or texture in a different way to non-autistic people; a mere hair on a sheet can cause physical pain to some. I always know if there is a hair loose on my back, or a rough seam inside a pair of trousers, for example. I will constantly scratch the area without knowing what is causing the irritation, often until it is red raw and sometimes until it bleeds.

Some fabrics, however, are completely the opposite and can cause me to take time stroking them. Velvet, for instance, is a most wonderful fabric – smooth one way, but stroke it in the opposite direction and it has a most satisfying texture. We autists often like to touch or to stroke certain fabrics just because they feel good. I would liken it to stroking a cat; some people find this satisfying because it feels nice, the cat fur is soft, and the repetitive action is calming.

Back in the room, I have to unpack immediately, even if it is just for one night. I put things away in cupboards and drawers and my toiletries in the bathroom. It gives me a sense of security knowing where everything is and that I have not forgotten anything. It allows me to relax.

Everything in my life has its own place, and being away from home is no different. I luxuriate in spending time just sitting, taking in everything around me, reading the menu from start to finish, and virtually tasting all the lovely foods I may choose during my stay. I love to take in sights, sounds, smells of hotel rooms; it is just like a full week's holiday for me without having to be away from home for so long.

Despite my preference for the familiar, I do try to step out of my comfort zone and not let my autistic sensory difficulties rule everything I do. Hotels and guest houses can be good places for being adventurous as stays in them are temporary, and I know I will be at home and safe again soon enough. An arranged work visit to Helsinki allowed me to stay in a wondrous hotel which I would never have chosen myself; the decoration was spectacular with interesting colours and textures – quite unlike other hotels I had visited. The most amazing sensory experience, although not directly related to the hotel, was the concept of daylight around the clock; that is, there was no night-time darkness, caused by Finland's northern location and the time of year. I was fascinated on the first night, looking out of my window at midnight and again at 2am to see daylight. I confess I did not get much sleep that first night; first, it was not dark enough and second, I was quite excited by this new experience.

While, on the whole, hotel restaurants and bars can be calming at certain times of the day (as discussed in Chapter 8), they can also be very busy and overbearing at peak times. They tend to be where business people and families let off steam after a day of meetings or sightseeing, and visitors treat them more as they would their own homes. That is, they relax more than in an ordinary restaurant and consequently make more noise without necessarily thinking about other customers.

Many people talking at the same time can be difficult because autists often find it hard to switch out background noises. What might be relatively quiet to non-autistic ears might sound like a jet engine to us. Imagine several working jet engines in a room at once and that is what it can be like. Immersing our focus into reading a book or listening to favoured music through headphones or ear buds can make this experience far more relaxing, and also stops other people trying to make small talk, which you know by now I am not friends with. If I am trying to unwind and relax, trying to take in someone else's conversation or personal issues just overloads my brain and I get very tired, very anxious or just irritated. I also find it really tough to hide disinterest or boredom, so I may come across as rude.

Some autists I know tend to avoid public areas in hotels, but I find other people fascinating to watch, so I try to spend at least a little time in them if I feel able to. In some places, I also find positive sensory experiences by looking around me at the variety of sensory stimulants: tall regal columns in hard, smooth marble which is cool to the touch, regal staircases, ornate gilt furniture, beautiful hand-knotted rugs and specially designed thick carpets which squelch when they are walked on. I love a luxury hotel for these stimulants, as well as the calming ambience, but I also get the feeling sometimes that there are unwritten rules or expectations, and I am scared I will fail the test. I am never quite sure if I am behaving or dressing the way I should. This fear of failure can be common in autistic individuals; we tend to like rules to be clearly set out.

My favourite type of accommodation is that with a homely feel which helps me to stay calm in a city, away from home. I love bookshelves with old, musty-smelling leather-bound books which inspire me to want to settle in for an afternoon's reading with a large mug or glass of something delicious and a blanket around me. A favourite is in New York: a hotel lived in for a few years by my idol Cary Grant – bonus!

It is also important to me that I stay in locations which make me feel more like a resident than a guest; I like to have a local market or grocery store nearby and feel safe walking around whatever the time of day, to feel part of the community. This reduces my likelihood of panicking when I am out and about. My sense of direction is not always great, especially if my senses are overloaded, so feeling safe outside the hotel is very important. Also if, for any reason, I become overwhelmed, I know exactly how to get back to my room quickly.

Being in the centre of a large city can get noisy if hotel windows are open, but for me that is part of the adventure: experiencing the sounds and smells of the city I am visiting. If everything was the same as at home, there would be little reason to travel. For some autistic individuals, however, the strange and frequent noises could potentially be excruciatingly painful. Many autists do not have a problem with loud noises if they are continuous, but sudden loud noises can cause what sounds like 'screaming' in their heads: fire or burglar alarms, horns beeping, trams, airplanes landing and so on. Headphones or ear buds really are the autist's best friend when he or she is travelling around different cities. I personally love hearing the sirens, the traffic zooming up and down the roads, the applause as street musicians entertain the crowds, the street traders shouting about their wares and the school children chattering as they climb into the school buses. I appreciate every sound and sight I experience as if it was my last, as some day it will be. Noise means a city is alive and that should always be exhilarating.

Smaller guest houses may be a better choice for some; they tend to be less busy, easier to find your way around and more peaceful. They are often interesting and quirky; many have small gardens or private sitting rooms for guests to relax in. One sensory challenge might be a tendency in some I have visited to fill rooms with bits and pieces which collect dust and can cause visual overload. This could cause a kind of motion sickness in autistic individuals. I have been known to put away as much clutter as possible into drawers and cupboards – even guides to the area, menus and other excess 'stuff' which is distracting. Simplicity is a preferred room décor style for the autistic senses; away from home, it can allow personal objects to be placed for comfort.

Another challenge here may be the need to share a large breakfast table with other guests; I have already discussed why this might be an issue for some autistic individuals. This is even worse than hotel breakfasts; it is a kind of forced socialising at the worst time of day for such an activity, for me at least.

Lastly, there might be a shared bathroom – a fear for my husband when travelling. He will only use a shower; he will never have a bath unless the tub is his own. He cannot bear the thought of bathing in a bathtub used by others. It is not simply the cleanliness but the fact that he has no idea who has been there before him. The thought makes him anxious to the point that he could physically vomit, or a full-blown autistic rage might ensue if someone tried to make him use it against his will. In every house he has lived in, he has replaced the bathtub, even if it appeared to be new. A person without this fear would never understand and think it extreme, but, for him, the fear is justified and logical. Our minds simply work in a way that is not always clear, either to us or to others.

Over the past couple of years, I have discovered another way to 'live' in a city: by renting an apartment short-term. These are rooms or suites within large buildings let out for any amount of time, from just one night to months at a time. They were a happy discovery for me, and whenever I travel alone to London, for example, I always rent a large apartment for however long I am staying. I am getting to know the area as a resident would, and I can grocery shop, cook my own meals, relax on the sofa or armchair, and generally feel as though I am home (except for my family, of course). On my last visit, I also had outside space in which to relax.

I was so excited the first time I stayed in one of these apartments. In the hallway I had my own pigeon hole (for any mail someone might want to send me), and there was a little hook by the kettle where I hung my keys. It was just like having my own little apartment in the city. I had independence, could cook my own food in my own kitchen, and I didn't have to socially engage with anyone or tip for room service. They are also in convenient locations, being easy walking distance from public transport, shops, restaurants and grocery stores. This one was close to a gym if I should so desire (I didn't), and had no less than six Indian restaurants nearby if I fancied popping out or having a takeaway in my apartment; I opted to dine in the only Chinese restaurant, the minute (literally) it opened, for a quiet experience.

It was definitely an opportunity to relax on my own in a large sensory-overwhelming city at the end of a busy day. There was no chatter of other guests, no bright hotel lights, and I could control my own apartment's temperature, which is very important, as I have discussed. Often autistic individuals take off their clothes when they can; children are known to just strip off anywhere, whereas adults mainly do so more appropriately behind closed doors. My husband will happily wear shorts and short sleeves all year round and at home hates wearing socks, shoes and trousers. He has been the same all his life, apparently. As an extreme, if he gets too cold, he would never put on extra clothes but turn up the heat until it is excruciatingly hot. A perfect balance of hot and cold is ideal. I can spend a winter's day inside taking layers of clothes off and on every few minutes and never feel quite right; it can be very tiring and very frustrating.

I have an autistic friend who travels a great deal for work and spends a lot of time in hotels. He doesn't like to eat in front of others (except for his own family) and therefore buys simple and cold foodstuffs to eat alone in his room. This apartment living would be ideal for him.

Wherever you might decide to stay in the city, there is just one thing I should mention which often catches me out: signs on toilet doors.

It is apparently clever to find different ways to label them. Men and women, gentlemen and ladies, guys and gals…but worse are the pictures: hats and shoes, pipe and lipstick, moustache and lips, stick and line drawings, silhouettes of heads, Batman and Wonder Woman, even toilets with seat up and seat down… As an autistic individual, I sometimes find visual clues difficult to interpret. I have entered a few men's toilets and got to the urinals before discovering my error. For non-autistic individuals, they must be confusing enough, but if I have difficulties interpreting body language or expressions, you can be sure I might have difficulties interpreting meaningless pictures which are supposed to highlight the difference between male and female toilets. Perhaps more toilets should simply be gender-neutral. Not only will we not have to interpret bizarre signs, they will be fairer for individuals who may not feel comfortable choosing one or the other. I am not an expert on this subject, but I know of many individuals who are transgender or non-binary, within and outside the autism community; they find it extremely uncomfortable and often threatening to choose one gender toilet over the other. Disabled toilets are usually gender-neutral; I see no reason to separate the non-disabled toilets.

If you are reading this and happen to work for a sign company or even a hotel, please encourage the decision-makers to stick to an easy method to distinguish the two, or simply change them to gender-neutral and save us all difficulties in interpretation.

Enjoy your stay, wherever it might be.

CHAPTER 11

AT ONE WITH NATURE

There is nothing I love more, in the centre of a city, than stepping out of the hubbub of the whirling, frenzied streets into green areas and being at one with nature. Somehow it instinctively slows us down, as we watch birds pottering around searching for food, butterflies skipping from bush to bush in a bid to relax and soak up the sun. Nature is healthy for body and mind; a chance to concentrate on ourselves, with no deadlines or rules.

There is always somewhere to escape to, where it is calmer, greener and more peaceful. Often there is the added bonus of water – perhaps a simple fountain or pond, or somewhere as noble as a lake or river. Although I revealed earlier that I don't like to travel on or be in the water, I love to watch: the gentle flowing of ripples or waves, the birds landing for a sip of liquid before soaring into the sky, children feeding ducks. If I want to relax in my own community, I often drive the short journey to the coast and sit on a bench high up over the sea to just watch. I love summer months where I can sit on the grass, under a large tree, taking shelter while I read or simply daydream, or watch canoes punt up and down the river.

There are so many wonderful parks and recreation sites in cities: Central Park in New York; Hyde Park, Regent's Park, Kensington Gardens, Hampstead Heath in London; Park Güell in Barcelona; Phoenix Park in Dublin – all great examples of nature in city centres. These, of course, are large and famous parks, but in addition there are many others, smaller, but equally useful to the autistic individual when escape or a calmer oasis is necessary.

The phrase 'tree hugging' has become synonymous with environmental campaigners who hug the trees to prevent them from being felled, and is often used in a derogatory way. However, science now backs up the premise that tree hugging is of benefit to health and wellbeing, and can be especially useful for individuals suffering with depression and to aid concentration. Just being around trees, plants and flowers feels hopeful, as if the world around us is an oasis of peace and calm.

If I am feeling overwhelmed at home, I try to spend time in the garden; just the simple task of weeding can be enough for me to slowly calm my mind. While weeding is my domain, if my husband has had an anxiety-ridden time in his office, he will always take a break to mow the lawn or go visit his hens for a chat.

Any aspect of nature is a natural calmer; parks are situated in cities for a reason. People need a break from chaos, and for autistic individuals, these places can be life-savers at times of need.

Central Park in New York has a double calming effect. Not only is it a park with plenty of trees and water sources, but it is also full of wildlife: squirrels running up and down trees, dogs everywhere being taken for walks, and a zoo for those who prefer animals to trees. I love to take a long walk around the myriad avenues within the 2.5-mile expanse of urban retreat.

Nature can be a wonderful source of sensory experiences for autistic individuals: the sounds alone are worth spending time with. I just love the cacophony of bird sounds heard: coos, chirps, tweets, chatters, quacks, warbles and trills. Plants and flowers provide the wondrous aromas of lavender, jasmine, rose, wisteria and the summer sweet pea. Many plants love to be touched, and for the autistic individual, this is an absolute pleasure. I love to run my hands over some plants – lavender for one, the curry plant another. They are visually and aromatically pleasing as well, so I have many of these in my own garden.

There is nothing I like better than wandering around a park in the autumn, when the sun is shining, the wind is blowing and I can take a walk among the falling leaves, kicking through the piles of leaves already relaxing on the ground, the swoosh of the crisp leaves against my feet.

Equally, in the summer I love the feel of grass under my bare feet, feeling at one with nature. As I write, the ground outside is wet and cold, and I long for the winter to turn into spring so that I can enjoy my garden to the full once more. I am hopeful: snowdrops and daffodils are beginning to rise from the ground ready to shine.

CHAPTER 12

RETAIL THERAPY

I have to confess: I love to shop. I am not sure it is always about the stuff to be bought. I just love the experience: stopping for a drink and a little read, watching people going about their day, finding a lovely lunch, picking up a bargain or two. But more and more I am finding, as the years go on, I simply don't have the patience to shop for as long I could once. I get so much more exhausted; my senses are battered to within an inch of their lives at times. I don't think it has anything to do with increased age, but I think shopping destinations are so much busier than perhaps 20 years ago. Globally, it seems we love to spend. I do still get the thrill of the chase, and occasionally come home with an unexpected item which excites me – usually a handbag or a beautiful notebook.

In an age where people across the world, including me, are now thinking about simplifying their lives and downsizing their 'stuff', much of the spending is not about buying things. It is often about going out simply to enjoy a cup of lovely frothy coffee or an indulgent pastry.

My favourite type of store, and one which I adore to visit, even if just for a coffee and a read, is a bookstore. I have loved books since the age of three: the feel, the smell, the taste (yes, I have been known to lick new paper and have had many paper cuts on my tongue), the temptation to turn to the end of a gripping crime plot, the spark of my imagination, often placing myself into the story. As a child, I was totally in love with Enid Blyton's works and dreamed of joining Chinky in the Wishing-Chair or being at the top of the Magic Faraway Tree. I was obsessed with the idea of boarding school and used to pack up my own tuck boxes of jam sandwiches and ginger beer. I wanted to join the Famous Five and become part of the Secret Seven. Even now as an adult, if I see one of these books, I start to read and am immediately taken back to childhood.

I have also reluctantly given in to the e-book age; for someone who loves to read, it is quick, convenient and easy on the back compared with having to lug around several books. But there is no greater thing than a physical book, with its bouquet of new freshly cut paper, the printing having an almost chemical aroma, and the crisp pages which crunch as they are turned. It is just as pleasing to smell a new book as to smell a fragrant Thai curry or a glass of full-bodied red wine. Paper generally is a wonderful material; I love the texture, the ability to scrunch it or tear it, and I will not even start to discuss my fascination for notebooks. I find nothing more satisfying when I am anxious or angry than tearing paper; the feel and the sound of it is very soothing. Other autistic people may find this sound painful, and you might see someone with hands cupped over their ears – trying to block out the sound of paper scrunching, for example, which they find extremely distressing.

Digital replacements just do not have the same sensory satisfaction – for me at least. My husband would say the complete opposite and his senses are satisfied completely by digital surrogates, but, as I remind you, all autists are different.

An indulgence in the city would be to have coffee in a bookstore, if possible sitting near a glass balcony so as to overlook shoppers, allowing me to wonder what customers are choosing: a novel to fire the imagination, a cook book to motivate the gastronomy, children's fiction to inspire a child's future. Being surrounded by books makes me feel nostalgic, animated, comfortable, inspired! People just seem to be calmer in a bookstore. While I mostly try to reign in my digressions, here I make no apologies for them. Books satisfy all of my senses, whether in reality or in the imagination. A coffee shop where I can focus on books is a delight and, together with the added bonus of wonderful aromatic lattes, hot chocolate and sweet sticky pastries, there are few places I enjoy more. I have dreamed about owning a children's bookstore, complete with children's café.

In contrast, giant shopping malls might just be the scariest places in which to shop, but paradoxically I find they are less exhausting in that all the stores are in one place, which prevents me from having to travel around a city, worrying about directions, transport and exhaust fumes.

My biggest terror in these large shopping malls is the number of retail outlets in the middle of the 'corridors' where enthusiastic and often desperate sales staff literally (and I don't use this word lightly) grab you as you walk by. They thrust pots of cream in your face or hair straighteners at you as they try to create an interest before you pull away. I have the dodging skills of a professional football player when I am trying to avoid walking within grabbing distance of these people. They just don't seem to be aware of the discomfort they create in some people. I hate anyone touching me when I am not expecting it, or getting too close and invading my space. It makes me so uncomfortable that I can get quite panicky and just want to get away. It can make me seem very rude in my haste to remove myself from the situation or I bump into everyone in my path.

Often I will wear my hair up so it can't be curled or straightened, wear nail polish so that my nails can't be scrutinised, and I have a good practised spiel about the phone, car and television channels I already have and why I don't need an upgrade. I always like to be prepared. Generally, I think autistic individuals spend a good deal of time getting prepared to face the non-autistic world: we pack headphones, we consider what food is available, what the lighting will be, have a multitude of maps and directions available to ensure we don't lose our way, plan journeys in fine detail to avoid any difficulties when it matters, are ready for changes in temperature and pack our comfort items. For me lip balm, notebook, pen and a squeeze object are a minimum must, as well as something to read.

I notice that as I get more tired, shops seem bigger, busier and brighter. I find it more challenging to find what I want and get irritated quickly. During a long trip to a mall, I couldn't find what I wanted in one large department store, so I dumped my basket in the middle of the store and walked out; it took me ten minutes, though, to find the exit and I became more and more hot and frustrated. This is usually when I bump into people a lot. When I am feeling more stressed, my coordination is affected and my senses are more acute than usual.

I could hear conversations around me, the whirring of the lights, a crying baby, the general buzz of a noisy environment, and I could smell doughnuts: chocolate, cinnamon, the sweet smell of sugar. I looked around but couldn't see any doughnuts. On my way out of the mall, I discovered the doughnut stand was a level down, directly below the department store, and I had smelt them from the floor above!

I love to wander in designer stores, not necessarily because I want to shop in them, but because the look of them gives me enormous visual pleasure. The items for sale are laid out neatly, usually colour-coded, with symmetrical displays, straight lines and clean layouts. Sweaters are folded perfectly, hangers are all the same way round, and nothing is out of place. There is rarely any chaos; music is low and gentle. These shops are an absolute delight to any pedant, or one who maintains obsessive order in their life. Handbag shops are my favourite – not because I love handbags, although I do, but because they are how I imagine my own collection: one on each shelf, being centre of attention, colours put together to complement. From a visual sensory perspective, these stores are pretty perfect and for me they are 'candy store' equivalents.

From other sensory perspectives, however, they can be the polar opposite. I might add that I am quite sure that they are not all the same, but I find many of these stores quite intimidating. It is not as if I cannot afford the products, but I get the feeling that staff are of the opinion I do not belong. Of course, this could be a misinterpretation of their body or facial language; it happens. If someone touches an item, a staff member will be there immediately, invading space and getting too close. Pathways seem to be blocked by sales assistants – keen to help or preventing ill-doing? I have been close to purchasing but usually walk out feeling extremely uncomfortable. I love to touch things, to feel the textures, to stroke items, but it seems in these stores this is frowned upon. It is such a shame as the items are of the quality where the feel of the fabric is exquisite, and I am sure more items would be sold if customers had the opportunity to touch these fabrics – whether clothes, leather or furniture. A soft leather handbag, for example, is made to be caressed. If an item doesn't feel good, I won't buy it. Their loss!

Autistic individuals love ordered or structured stores. One such store, a worldwide technology store, is a joy: spacious, quiet, low lighting, and everything placed just so. Staff quietly walk around, helping people at computers and sitting quietly chatting about a device to be purchased or repaired.

On one occasion, when I wanted to head for a higher floor in the store, I discovered that one of my sensory nightmares was about to come true. The looming staircase was made solely from glass. I am afraid of heights, so seeing through the stairs down the various levels was a step too far. After a lot of persuading, I did manage to get to the level I needed, especially when I was told I could use the lift coming back down. Then I found out that the lift was also made of glass. Inspired by Roald Dahl's *Charlie and the Great Glass Elevator* perhaps, but I was paralysed with fear. All around me were people tutting, as I was glued to the spot, not knowing which way to look. By the time I had managed to get back down the stairs, with my husband's support, I could feel my heart pumping so fast that I was scared it would pop out of my chest.

By this time, the enormity of the experience overcame me and I felt myself going into a meltdown situation. I knew I was shaking, and I was feeling nauseous and hot. I had to sit down for a while to calm myself before I could leave the store some 20 minutes later. Surrounding a store in glass seems to be a trend and one that I shall try to avoid. For others who enjoy transparency, it might be the most amazing experience ever, and on their behalf I appreciate the architecture of such different interior design.

There are many experiences I have which I appreciate for what they are; I may not always like them or want to engage with them, but I always try to notice and appreciate what I see. This is the way we learn to enjoy new things, and as I know one of my weaknesses is a propensity to stick to what I know, this appreciation is important for my self-development as an individual, regardless of autism.

Department stores or supermarkets provide yet more challenges for autists. The location of goods, and even departments, seem to be forever changing. I know, of course, that this is a marketing ploy to encourage people to walk around items they don't usually need to find items they do need. But for us, it is most annoying and frustrating. I know where I expect things to be, and sudden changes can affect my senses of balance and direction, and cause my body temperature to change rapidly. I often get hot and nauseous, and need to get out quickly. I sometimes have to touch the products on the shelves just to satisfy my visual perception of where things are. If I get particularly anxious, I have been known to count things to 'see them' – loaves of bread on a supermarket shelf, for example.

Department stores are usually bright and busy, so feeling disorientated in one can be a discernible sensory challenge. Bright lights can frequently cause extreme pain in the eyes or head for autistic individuals. Often there is a low buzz, which for us can sound as loud as a police siren. The combination can be unbearable. There are so many paths to take around and through the store. How to choose? Do I follow the more obvious paths and bump into people, or weave my way through the various departments and risk bumping into rails or browsing customers? The first department often is beauty and perfumes; there seems to be a host of sales staff ready to squirt you with the latest perfume – a nightmare for someone who is so sensitive to many aromas. If I catch the wrong scent, my eyes swell up, my face itches and my head aches for hours. It doesn't take long to react, either.

If I could plan these stores in a way that would make them more customer-friendly and, even more so, autistic-customer-friendly, I would suggest different zones or departments to be colour-coded with large swinging coded signs above so that they can be seen without walking around; the flooring would also be colour-coded. I also think there should be one-way systems to save bumping into people. Perhaps these are ideals for me alone, but you never know, someone may take notice…one day. There may even be such a store which I have not yet discovered.

I love to visit supermarkets where fruits and vegetables are laid out beautifully, in rows or diagonal lines. Items are placed next to each other according to colour and shape. The look of the produce is so appealing that I just want to pick it up and eat it there and then. If only more stores took advantage of the senses being so closely linked. Sight, smell and touch especially are so important for selling food because you can't generally use taste at the selling stage. I love to see stores where outside there are lines and lines of coloured juicy fruit and vegetables, whether they are grocery stores on the city streets in the USA, or market stalls around the world where goods are laid out to make best use of colour and attract the buyers to them. Autistic eyes adore such order and neatness, but appreciation of such beautiful arrangements, I guess, is not limited to us alone, although not being non-autistic it is difficult for me to know for sure.

I also love homeware stores where there are piles of coloured towels, bed linen, cushions, pillows and pans, and stationery stores with perfect rows of pens and pencils, folders and paper. Everything is colour-coded and neatly arranged. You will have gleaned by now that colour coding is one of my favourite things – why wouldn't you love it? It makes life pretty and so much easier to navigate.

There are times in these large stores, however, when I get overwhelmed by the crowds of people, the various aisles, departments and exits. There is so much choice that it can become difficult to make a decision. I often find myself just wandering, a little zombie-like, and bumping into people and displays, overwhelmed by the chattering and the bustle. My balance gets worse, I try to avoid any people contact, and even the quietest of store music sounds like a big drum being banged in my head. In stores I know quite well, I'm always aware of the toilet's locality; these can be places of respite away from the chaos if needed, and if I am unable to get out of the store quickly. I also turn back to mantra or visualisation exercises. These can be done quietly and do not have to be visible to others. They can be extremely useful and are definitely comforting. I have seen individuals in large stores wearing headphones – not just little ear buds but large headphones – and sometimes they do not appear to be attached to a music device or mobile phone. These will often be autistic individuals or others who have sensory processing issues; the headphones allow them to do normal activities while shutting out the sounds of chaos.

Outside, I love a good bustling market. There are so many aromas: soap, incense, fried foods, candy, sweat, flowers and the heat or chill of the air. Often the combination makes my nose itch and beg for respite. Markets are great for people watching; they are places where all ages, classes and nationalities come together and grab a bargain. They tend to be noisy places: lots of chattering and shouting from the vendors selling their wares. I don't mind this shouting, but I do object when they try to stop you walking and use heavy sales tactics to persuade you to buy, even when it is obvious you don't want to. This just makes me feel uncomfortable, as it does in the shopping centres. I don't want to be physically grabbed, nor do I want someone coming too close and invading my personal space. The other maddening thing is being bumped into, mostly because people are avoiding others bumping into them. Perhaps everyone in markets is disorientated and loses coordination? Perhaps markets are places where equity is rampant, where differences don't matter? I certainly get disorientated when markets are busy and have a tendency to veer off into people and objects. 'Sorry' seems to be my mantra here.

And I just love the colours of a market. Whether it is beautiful flowers, food, crafts, antiques, gifts or just general bric-a-brac, the rainbow of colours and textures are simply splendid – an artist's palette to be treasured.

Wherever I am shopping, there is one regular event which I really loathe: sales of any kind. I cannot bear to walk into a store and find rails and rails of items which have no relation to each other, are not colour-coded and in many circumstances are not even arranged so that sizes or like products are together. Items are placed in bins or there are goods together which don't belong. I hate to rummage; the stores where they heavily discount designer goods are not my friends as I only find bargains if I spend a lot of time rummaging. I simply don't have the patience for this. Also there is a tendency to be touched as another shopper rummages alongside me or grabs an item at the same time as me. Online sales are much easier. Stores in sales time are, of course, far busier as well, and I become overloaded easily and have to leave.

Just a few years ago, it wasn't a problem; sales were at the end of summer and the beginning of the year. Now, however, there always seems to be a sale on somewhere. There are even pre-sale sales. It seems people don't like to shop unless they are getting a bargain. Why don't stores charge less to start with and never have sales? This would suit me well, and many others, I am sure.

After the sales, it's definitely time to relax…and where better than a spa?

CHAPTER 13

RELAX

After all the chaos and stress of shopping, a lovely indulgent experience in a spa is just what I need.

I absolutely adore having facials, foot and hand massages, pedicures and manicures. There are certain parts of my body that love to be pampered; I love an Indian head massage, for example. I find the firm pressure is quite calming; it follows the same principle as the squeeze machine, invented by Temple Grandin, to calm her cattle. A trip to the hairdresser is not complete without the pressured head massage as she washes my hair. Woe betide her, however, if she dares to splash a drop of water near my face. I turn from a pussy cat into a tiger in a split second. Equally, I like firm pressure on my feet and love a reflexology session for this reason.

A friend, also autistic, loves deep tissue massages, hot rocks, cupping, or whatever the latest kind of massage is, but I couldn't bear it on my torso. My husband loves firm pressure, but he says it is actually painful to him to have light touch applied or even a light breath on his skin. Many people dislike having their feet and heads touched for whatever their reason. Each one of us has valid reasons for what we like and don't like, although they might not seem logical to one who does not have the same sentiments.

I also love having the creams and hot flannels applied during a facial, although an important caveat to remember is to visit the loo before the facial, even if you don't need to. I suffered an entire hour wishing it was over so I could get up – what a waste of money and a good facial. Another time, I think I must have fallen asleep near the end because suddenly it was over and I was being offered a glass of water and my robe. Facials for me are the ultimate sensory pleasure: that of touch in a calming environment.

Therapists take note, though: the room *must* be calm and peaceful for us autists. We don't want bright pink walls (yes, I have seen them) or bubbling brook music (which just hastens the need for the loo). We don't want strongly scented incense either; I have acute sensitivities with many aromas, and incense ruins the experience for me. I do love some aromas: lavender, vanilla, lemongrass… Perhaps ask the customer in advance if she or he has any preference or any allergies. I also have to avoid any lotions and potions scented with rose, so I always mention this. It is a shame because I love to smell roses in the garden, just not lingering on my skin. Too many sensory encounters, as listed here, will likely cause sensory overload and counteract the relaxation expected – and indeed promised – during a spa experience.

Of course, there are many other experiences at a spa: the pool (which I avoid due to my neurotic fear of getting water near my face), the hot tub (which I might use if I am alone or with my husband, but not with strangers in case of water splashes), the sauna (why would anyone want to sit in a box and sweat, particularly someone who finds extreme heat a sensory nightmare?) and often the gym. Why spoil a perfectly good spa experience by ending it with a gym workout? A yoga or meditation session would be lovely and calming, but pumping weights in a smelly room full of other potentially smelly people! Why?

In every city, there is a growing trend for nail bars – an opportunity to take a break from frenzied shopping, to get your nails looking their best. While I don't mind a manicure, I worry about whether the nail technician will expect to sit and chat throughout. I would rather have silence and lovely music in the background, but experience tells me they mostly engage in small talk – not my idea of a relaxing half hour. At the hairdressers, I can read to avoid small talk; during a facial, I just close my eyes and pretend I'm asleep. I have not yet found a way to avoid it during a manicure!

For my next birthday, I have plans to visit, alone, a beautiful yoga and spa retreat in a country I have yet to determine. What could be more perfect? Relaxing without having to talk to anyone, energising or relaxing yoga sessions, meditation, delicious healthy food, waking to stunning scenery, walking, reading, having treatments and noting inspirations. No need to think about anything else at all (except to miss my family).

There is much to be said for appreciating the simple things in life, and for an autistic individual who often spends time being anxious, angry or overwhelmed, a simpler lifestyle could be the answer. Fewer things around them creates more calm, fewer people creates more peace, good-quality food and calming activities inspire a healthy body and mind.

CHAPTER 14

BODY BEAUTIFUL

In the city, there are a multitude of options for keeping the body beautiful. Most evident are probably the numerous chains of gyms which pop up on street corners, in shopping arcades and in leisure complexes.

I have joined many gyms over the years and usually go for about two weeks before I get bored and leave again, having paid a year's subscription and bought uncomfortable lycra and neon trainers. I am not alone, of course, but a gym is somewhere I don't feel comfortable but feel obliged to visit for the sake of my physical body. I get anxious in gyms, with the complicated-looking equipment, where sweaty bodies sit and grunt as weights are pushed and pulled. Even worse, I often have to watch myself exercise in a mirror; this can confuse my sense of direction and balance. A quick wipe down with a towel cannot remove all the germs and sweat from the equipment, and it seems to me to be so unhygienic. With my acute sense of smell, the aroma here is often painful and so bad sometimes I can physically taste the smell or feel nauseous. Many machines here – for example, the running machines – can be a danger if, like many autistic individuals, you are prone to loss of balance, lack of coordination or motion sickness. For others, the repetitive movements of such machines might actually satisfy the body's need for certain motions – akin to stimming for comfort. As with all experiences, there are autistic individuals who may love them and others who will despise them. We are a heterogeneous community in the same way that non-autistic individuals are, and this should never be forgotten.

I have danced all my life (my mum said I danced before I was born), and except for a short break in my teens due to illness, I have been to classes of some sort regularly. Cities tend to house a few dance academies of various disciplines, as well as the larger dance colleges and companies in some. Despite my poor balance and coordination in many areas of my life, it has always been different when I am dancing. My brain seems to light up when the music comes on and allows my body to move naturally. I used to compete and loved the sparkle of the costumes and the trophies. I might avoid social occasions with small groups of people, but put me on the dance floor or a stage with hundreds of people watching and I come alive; it is as comfortable to me as my home. Had I not suffered with arthritis at the age of 14 and been in hospital for months, I would probably have gone on to make dance my career; I did qualify as a dance teacher at least. Dance gives so many benefits: it can boost the mood, energise, calm you down, release pent-up emotions, create a safe place for expression of feelings, promote self-awareness and self-esteem, and help coordination and balance.

I have also been practising and teaching karate for 26 years. I discovered many years ago that martial arts and autism can go hand in hand to work with and help each other, especially in overcoming some of the common sensory differences. Martial arts can help physically with issues including coordination, balance, judging speed and distance, stamina, flexibility and sense of direction. Classes are usually very structured, which is good for autistic lovers of routine and rules, and movements are repetitive, which is important to many autists. Martial arts give individuals confidence by encouraging a stronger mind and body as well as increasing technical ability; for autistic individuals, this confidence is often key to coping with difficult or uncomfortable situations including bullying, which sadly occurs for many individuals who have differences or who may appear vulnerable or weak in some way. If you are interested in exploring these links further, you might want to read my book *Autism and Martial Arts: A Guide for Children, Parents and Teachers* (2015).

I discovered yoga in 2014 as a result of my annual ritual of pre-birthday anti-ageing research. After one class with a wonderful teacher, I was in love with it and I have never looked back.

Yoga is not, as many people expect to be, all about wrapping your legs around your head and standing on your hands. Of course, the physical postures are one of the main reasons many people take up yoga. For me, physically I wanted to become stronger and more flexible, but I also wanted more. I have been blessed to have a teacher who concentrates on the other aspects of yoga equally, and for me these have become more important. These include our attitude to the world and ourselves, breathing practice, looking inwards at our selves, concentration, meditation and enlightenment. To many people, these concepts seem completely alien and idealistic. However, it is surprising how much of yoga philosophy can be practised in daily life without much effort and certainly without any whiff of religion.

As well as strengthening my body, I have found yoga to be helpful in shaping the way I think. I use the breathing and meditation practices to control my anxieties, very useful, for instance, when I am about to walk on stage at a conference to talk about autism. When my brain is close to overload, I have the ability to sit quietly with a short visualisation exercise. Although it doesn't always clear the overload completely, it certainly helps. My feeling is that the more and more I practise, the easier it will be to handle the loss of control my autism sometimes causes. I use my yoga practice to try to control my habits: of getting anxious just because someone has a water pistol nearby (it's not worked yet, but I am hopeful), of getting annoyed when the dishwasher is not loaded in the way I like it, of staying calm when someone pulls out in front of me while I am driving.

I do find some aspects of class unsettling, though; my senses get the better of me when I can't balance well, figure out where parts of my body are meant to be, or get dizzy when I am practising an inversion (where my head is below my heart). I also get anxious if there are hairs on my mat, when the sun is shining in my eyes, or when someone else has taken my usual mat space; it took me a year to start to interact with other yogis in the class.

I am a firm believer now that yoga and its various concepts will find you when you are ready for it, and as a coping strategy for autism it is a bonus find. I am glad it found me. It has certainly changed my sensory perceptions in some aspects of my life and made me appreciate more what I have. After three years of classes, I have also completed an intense foundation course and will shortly be starting my teacher training diploma. It really has shaped my life, and breath control and meditation has helped me with many sensory and general autistic difficulties. My future classes will be aimed towards individuals like me, who need respite from the daily grind, relief from pressures (e.g. anxiety, stress) or health issues. In India, yoga in all its forms is relied upon to ensure long and healthy lives. Inspiring!

CHAPTER 15

HEALTH IS VITAL

Hospitals are everywhere in cities and are a place most people experience in some way at some point in their lives. Whether patient or visitor, having a baby or comforting a relative, checking on a worry or going through intensive treatments or surgery, whatever the reason for the visit, hospitals hold a whole host of sensory challenges. You already know from the Introduction that I have been in and out of hospitals for a large part of my life. I worked in various hospitals over a period of about 15 years. I have been a patient with various illnesses and conditions, had nasty but necessary drugs and surgeries, and had numerous blood tests and investigations. I have been through tunnels for scans, received regular finger prick tests, hoping for a good result so that I could be injected with ghastly drugs, seen uncountable images of my insides, been stapled, cut into, prodded, poked, stretched and pummelled. I once punched a physiotherapist for pummelling my chest when I had just come out of surgery having had two ribs removed (I was nine years old). I was awake (but dozy) while my hip was pulled apart, resurfaced and put back together again. It is safe to say I have had my fair share of unpleasant experiences in hospitals.

For many people entering a hospital for the first time, the smell is probably the first thing they notice. The majority of hospitals have a tendency to smell very medicinal: a combination of antiseptic and disinfectant together with heat. I find this smell comforting; it is a smell I have experienced since childhood and it offers a safety blanket against the world.

I have had many sensory experiences in hospitals, and not all of them have been disagreeable. Hospitals are very bright; they are usually painted mostly white or very light colours to give that clean and sanitised look. Although I might not normally like such décor, in a hospital it is strangely reassuring. One modern-day change to hospitals is the increasing use of glass. I have already outlined another of my experiences with glass in a store; many hospitals are going the same way as they update their buildings. Perhaps it is supposed to be more open, less stuffy, but I for one don't like it.

My husband cannot stand to be in a hospital; it makes him want to thrash out and he can barely breathe. On one occasion, he was admitted to casualty with a suspected heart attack after intentionally crashing his truck into a lamppost (he had experienced chest pains which turned out to be muscular and stress-related, and was avoiding driving headlong into another vehicle). In a hospital, he feels he has no control; there are people everywhere screaming, calling and rushing about. He is in a close confined space behind a curtain, not knowing what is happening. He hates to stay there longer than he has to. On that occasion, one doctor told him he could go, so he was all ready to leave when another doctor came by and requested he stay and have more tests. It was not a pretty sight; he got so anxious and it made him angry. I could tell he was about to go into a rage, and I explained to a nurse why this was happening. We managed to calm him down eventually and get him to move into a bed in another area where it was quieter, until he could leave. In fact, he had to stay overnight in the observation ward; he refused to take off his coat or even his shoes, or to eat or drink for the entire time he was there. He was just so stressed and unhappy. The lights were bright and the monitor he was attached to beeped and flickered all night; together with the activity from staff and other patients and visitors, he was just so overwhelmed that he withdrew from all communication completely. It was a couple of weeks before he recovered from the experience…if ever!

Following a whiplash injury last year, he was called in for an MRI scan. This is where you go through a tunnel, which is magnetic, while the machine takes slice photos of the area being scanned. It is also horrendously noisy; patients are usually advised to take music to be played through headphones. Within a couple of minutes of the scan starting, he went into sensory meltdown and had what was probably a panic attack: jumping up, screaming and shouting to get out of there. He has since had similar episodes when he has been in a situation out of his control. Given a choice, he would never go near a hospital again.

Hospitals, of course, can be scary places for individuals not used to them, and with autistic senses being so acute for many, staff should be trained to know how to support these patients. There should be facilities to dim the lights, or even eye masks provided in sleep areas, to at least allow patients to get some rest, and perhaps some ear plugs to block out the noises which may be unsettling. If you are a scheduled in- or out-patient, you can prepare for these visits to some degree, but for some the experience is still unpleasant, to put it mildly. For emergency visits, there is little one can do to prepare.

As an experienced in-patient, there are a few things I pack first to ensure a more comfortable stay:

- lip balm (wards get hot and dry)
- face and body lotion (see first item)

- ketchup (to hide the taste of some meals) and snacks

- dry shampoo (nothing worse than the feel of bad hair)

- lots of books (makes everything feel better)

- notebook and pen (my always items, whatever the situation)

- eye mask (shields bright lights and enables you to avoid talking when you don't feel like it).

I would probably add ear buds or headphones for others.

Each autistic individual will react differently, but it is highly likely there will be some kind of acute discomfort, in addition to the reason they are there. Staff should be prepared for some communication difficulties if the individual is badly affected by sensory issues.

I should like to think that autistic awareness is more prevalent in such places; sadly, this is not necessarily so. There are, though, some wonderful staff, who do an incredible job in difficult circumstances.

ENTERTAINMENT

'The true work of art is but a shadow of the divine perfection.'

Michelangelo

CHAPTER 16

SHOWBIZ

The theatre is where I feel most comfortable. I have performed on the stage many times myself, mainly dancing, with a little acting thrown in on occasion. I am a woman of extremes. I can be painfully anxious about some situations; walking into a room of strangers, even in small numbers, can be excruciatingly painful for me. I can be so anxious that I lose all sense of direction and balance, and bump into anything or anyone in my way. Yet, performing on stage in front of an audience of hundreds is for me exciting and where I feel at home. Of course, I always get a little nervous while I am standing in the wings waiting to enter the stage, but once I go on, I seem to transform into another person: confident, exuberant and excited. Perhaps it is about putting on an act – and not being judged for myself but for the character I become. Perhaps it is inherited, as my dad is the same. Despite sensory differences in other situations, I love the stage lights, the heat which comes from them, the complete blackness as I look into the audience. I also love to visit the theatre – for plays, musicals, ballets…anything really.

It is always difficult to know what a theatre show will entail – how many sensory challenges will it bring with it? I am normally pretty safe with a ballet, for example, but for some other shows I have watched, I'd have sooner been more prepared.

Recently, I had the pleasure of watching *The Curious Incident of the Dog in the Night-Time*. This show is based on the award-winning novel by Mark Haddon, and is narrated by a young man who has Asperger's Syndrome.

Ironically, the show started with a bang: there were sudden loud noises and bright flashing lights which went on for a few minutes, as well as bright white boxes all over the stage. I was so uncomfortable that I thought I was going to have to leave the theatre without even watching the show. Then suddenly it all stopped and it went quiet. The show was incredible and so clever, and my senses were paradoxically shattered yet excited. People moved all about the stage acting as both actors and objects. They became buses and trains, patterns and simple objects such as cubes.

Although I loved the show, I do think it should have come with a warning from the beginning about the sensory challenges. Not only was it difficult for any autistic individual in the audience, but I should think for someone with epilepsy, for example, it could have proved dangerous. If I saw it again, I would take a blindfold for the first five minutes of the show. I would rarely avoid a sensory encounter completely, because it might be positively spectacular, but if I was pre-warned, I could prepare myself, mentally getting ready for it along with more practical solutions such as ear plugs.

On a musical theatre visit, my senses were overcome and this ruined a lovely evening. I was seated next to a gentleman who, without meaning to be rude, was extremely large; his legs were taking up all of my space and the space of the person on the other side of him. Worse, though, was his personal aroma. I tried to ignore it, and tried covering my nose with a scarf, but by the second half of the show the smell was so bad I really thought I would vomit. The theatre was pretty warm and, combined with the summer's evening, the smell worsened over the period of two and a half hours.

I ended the evening with an excruciatingly bad headache in combination with the nausea.

At the end of the show, the audience moved very slowly from the theatre, and as we were three tiers up, we joined the queue to descend the only stairs in the theatre. The journey took some 20 minutes, and there was a lot of noise, a lot of jostling and bumping into people. It was uncomfortable and caused my husband to go headlong into a full meltdown fuelled by discomfort and increased body heat, resulting in an immense rage. He finally stormed out of the theatre, bumping into numerous people on the way out, and I will just say the rest of the evening went downhill from there onwards.

I learned two things that evening: never book a seat at any level except the bottom one so that we don't have to go up or down any stairs and get stuck in crowds, and always take a bottle of essential oil which can be sniffed as necessary to disguise any bad smells; I think nose pegs would be taking it too far! I have been known on previous occasions to move seats if someone with particularly strong perfume is sitting nearby, but in this case the theatre was completely full.

To the non-autistic person, the experience would have ended at the final bow; for us it lasted for days, and even now if I book theatre tickets, I worry from beginning to end in case history repeats itself. I anticipate problems and prepare to prevent them. There is not much to prepare, though, when it is other people who cause the problems; they are out of my control, regrettably.

The city is the best place to be for one of my favourite types of show; I love a good musical: *The Phantom of the Opera, Chitty Chitty Bang Bang, Oliver!* (many times), *Cats, Starlight Express, Me and My Girl*...my absolute favourite is *The King and I*. I just adore the glitz and glamour of it all – the sensory spectacle of the beautiful costumes, the songs and dances. This, for me, feeds the senses in every way. Visually, it is stunning with the costumes and choreography; aurally, the music is dramatic and rhythmic, which sits well with me; and, most importantly, the artistic creativity really lights up my heart, as they use simple fabrics to give the illusion of calm waters and rainstorms, mountains and forests, and steps to give the illusion of running. Although I am in the audience and far away, I can see the textures used and visualise myself touching them. The attention to detail is amazing, and this is important for most autistic individuals, as we connect to each detail more than the overall 'picture'.

As an autistic individual, I would always find out in advance if any surprises were likely to be part of the performance: in *Phantom*, for example, the chandelier drops suddenly, which could be too much of a shock for many of us. Similarly, a car comes down from the eaves during *Chitty Chitty Bang Bang*. Although we often find it difficult to deal with sensory surprises, preparing ourselves mentally for possibilities helps ease the experience. Of course, specific surprises may affect autistic individuals in different ways. I would turn to jelly and tears in seconds if water or a custard tart was thrown at me. I cannot explain why the discomfort of mess causes me such complete panic and even physical pain; my whole body feels stiff and my heart rate increases, and therefore my brain cannot always fathom what is happening.

Theatre experiences can be a complete no-no for many autistic individuals: large crowds, hot and cold temperatures, loud noises and often flashing lights, being close to strangers and often being bumped into, unfamiliar sounds and aromas. We are all so different that nothing can be assumed when sensory experiences are taken into consideration. The worst sensory experience for me at theatres (and lots of other public venues more and more) is the hand dryers in the toilets. They seem to have been made more powerful, and they make a dreadful whooshing sound. I walk in the door with my hands over my ears and as far as possible they remain there. I keep hand-wipes or waterless cleansing gel with me so that I can exit the loo and go straight out of the door, cleaning my hands when I get outside. I find the noise goes straight through my head and causes my ears to be pained and my body to vibrate.

I have been to some fantastic plays which offer a very different sensory experience. Whereas the musicals tend to be loud and bright, plays on the whole tend to be more laid-back and low-key. Often they are in smaller theatres, which works well for me. There is less likelihood I will get lost between my seat and the bar or the loo. I can familiarise myself with logistics more quickly; thus, I am more comfortable. The actors' voices are a little quieter, and the story gives more structure as there is no stopping at regular points to burst into song and dance. There are different sensory challenges at some plays. One horror play included many sudden noises, screams and pungent aromas: dust, must, heat, cold air – all very authentic. I was prepared for most of these, however, so I was not unduly affected by them. I find the smell of 'cold' to be very earthy and satisfying – like the chill of late-autumn air.

Local to where I live is a small community theatre which houses a local amateur dramatics group. Although just outside a city, I am including this to highlight the comparisons with the bigger theatres and how I, as an autistic adult, experience the two.

Together with my husband, I watch at least five theatre productions here each year. There are pros and cons, as with any form of entertainment. The theatre is very small, having seating for 70 in the audience. The theatre has a little semi-circular stage, and the basic scenery is changed for each production: colour, curtains, rugs, furniture and accessories. Over the few years we have been coming here, I have seen most cast members appear time and time again. The audience varies, but we see the same faces often. When, for me and many autistic individuals, the feeling of comfort comes with familiarity, this can be very positive. I know where everything is, when it starts, how quickly to run at the interval to get first in the refreshments queue.

I enjoy watching some actors who are perhaps not so polished – a few fluffed lines, and occasionally a mysterious voice echoes from backstage to prompt a silent actor. If it happens too often – and it has from time to time – I get the giggles. Many in the audience are elderly, and with it being a small theatre, they are not shy to call out or speak loudly to their neighbour who perhaps hasn't noticed. The cast–audience engagement is different in this theatre – more informal somehow. The sights and sounds are much closer, and these bring an invitation to be a part of the performance in some way. This can work the other way, though, and some audience members continually talking can be very annoying; at one performance, Joe stopped me walking over and telling them to be quiet. As autistic individuals may find it difficult to filter background and foreground noises, having the audience chatting can drown the sounds of the actors.

I love this theatre so much now that I am preparing to tread the boards once more, in the pantomime; it will be my turn to forget my lines!

There are negatives everywhere in life; I try to focus on what is good. If I need to calm myself at the theatre, there is usually one fairly easy way to do this. Most theatre seats are covered with a velvet-like fabric. As you may remember, this is a little obsession of mine. Velvet has the most perfect texture: comforting, sensual, smooth but rough, a tactile rainbow of sorts. Rainbows always calm me.

I shall take my final bow and move on to another love of mine.

CHAPTER 17

IN THE DARK

There are a few things I consider to be indulgences in my life, and one of them is undoubtedly going to the cinema on my own during the day. I can completely switch off from the world (no phones allowed) and not have to worry about anything except which flavour popcorn to eat or, if I am in the States, whether to buy Milk Duds or Whoppers. It seems wrong somehow to visit the cinema alone, but I think that's why I love it.

I try always to sit in the back corner seat. This means no one is sitting behind me, I don't get disturbed, and there is often a little ledge at the side of the seat on which to put my bag (I like to be tidy). I can also see everyone who comes in and everything around me. While the lights are still on, I can people-watch, and when they are turned off, I feel safer knowing someone can't sneak up on me. Also, I prefer to sit around the edges so that I know exactly where my physical body is positioned. The only other place I would comfortably sit would be in the centre; symmetrical to both sides. These days, I usually book online so that I can get my preferred seat, but even so I always sit down really early. I like to settle myself and get comfortable. If I arrived after lights out, my sense of direction would be affected, even though I sit in the same place. This would potentially cause me to lose balance and become uncoordinated. Once I was seated, I would feel unsettled throughout the entire film. Having thermoception differences, I am prepared for every temperature eventuality: dressed in layers ready to overcome both the heat and the chilly air conditioning. Just in case I need to see in the dark or check my watch, I use a tiny keyring torch, purchased solely for cinema use.

I manage to get excited by a singing hotdog! It heralds anticipation of the experience to come. I love it when the lights are dimmed and it all goes silent. Then the surround sound booms, the picture almost engulfing me in its gargantuan proportions. In one cinema chain, however, I am forced to cover my eyes and ears as the ident leading up to the movie is not, for me at least, autism-friendly. It starts as waves of water, which splash and then solidify into an image of the cinema seats being stitched, before splashes and little balls make pretty and very noisy patterns zooming in and out, all over the screen, finishing with flashing images which turn into the logo at the end. The images are very bright and very loud. For the hyposensory autist, however, this ident may just be a welcome sensory stimulant.

There are occasions when I hide my face behind my scarf if the image on the screen seems to get too close, but movies always seem to be better on a big screen. I remember watching a Harry Potter movie with my niece many years ago. I was fascinated by the fantasy Quidditch game, the children all zooming about in the air on broomsticks chasing little balls. It all sounded so realistic and it felt as though they were flying all around our heads. It almost made me want to duck if they came near to me; in fact, I confess I actually did, in the same way I lean when I am driving around a sharp bend. These sounds and sights can cause sensory overload in some autistic individuals and can result in loud outbursts of anxiety or rage. There are increasingly frequent 'autism-friendly' performances at cinemas, where these behaviours can be reduced by lower lights and reduced volume, no trailers before the main movie, and more flexibility in taking your own food and drinks, and being able to move around during the performance. An advantage of my penchant for daytime viewing is that often I am nearly or completely alone in the movie theatre. If I am alone, sometimes I wander around, trying out different seats to find the best one – hence my current favourites.

I never want to leave when the film is over; I would happily sit there all day, and if a movie came on that I didn't care for, I could have a snooze. Now that would be an indulgence – perhaps I should suggest day passes so I could wander between screens all day!

CHAPTER 18

FANCY A DRINK?

I met my lovely husband in a nightclub; despite his autism (at that time unknown), he worked as a doorman for a few years. Perhaps I picked up on his quietness, the fact that he was so different to the rest of the nightclub staff in a way I couldn't identify at the time. He is of the view that it was fate; we were apparently meant to meet and discover the autistic world together. Perhaps this is true. In theory, nightclubs would be the last place to find autistic individuals – noisy, bright and smelly (at that time smoking was allowed and sweat was an ever-present aroma, together with many strong perfumes), flashing lights, the 'evil' smoke machine, crowds of people getting too close and touching accidentally (and sometimes not accidentally!), a social environment... There are many opportunities for sensory differences to result in excessive anxiety, aggression and withdrawal, making individuals vulnerable in an atmosphere which may be prone to negative alcohol- or possibly drug-fuelled behaviour – even violence.

Many autistic individuals stand too close to others, have difficulties judging personal space and find navigating a room full of people and obstructions difficult. This may put them at risk if they upset the wrong people. Even a visit to the bathroom is not relaxing, as experience reminds me that they are usually filled with women making up, or, later in the evening, throwing up.

For some, however, they are a place to meet 'friends'. I say it in that way, because in my experience 'friends' isn't always the right word. I know of an autistic individual who is happy to go to nightclubs and bars alone. She is happy to buy people she meets there drinks, and share everything she has, and this means people talk to her and she has new 'friends'. Outside of the clubs and bars, these people take advantage of her, borrow large sums of money without ever paying them back, and lead her into all kinds of situations where she is not really safe. She has no idea because they are her 'friends'. People laugh at her, make comments about her, but she is completely oblivious to these people. They have no effect on her because her 'friends' remain 'friendly'. It makes me very sad that there are individuals who are happy to take advantage of vulnerable people to get what they want. I hope that some of these people really are her friends and that they care about her in some way. She is not willing to listen to anyone who tries to intervene.

Autistic individuals may be impulsive and easily distractible; many will find social situations so difficult that they will trust anyone who shows an interest or seemingly shares a passion. Bars and clubs need to be negotiated carefully, especially with the rise of spiked drinks and illegal substances. Autistic internal senses are often naive and need to be supported in certain 'at risk' environments.

The worst thing about clubs, in my opinion, is the hen, stag or equivalent party, or other large groups of individuals celebrating raucously. The mix of excitement, copious amounts of alcohol and a willingness to let go of all inhibitions can be a sensory nightmare for anyone on the spectrum. With drunkenness, or just overexcitement, comes loss of control. High levels of noise – laughter, talking, screaming; falling over and bumping into people around them; pushing and shoving; embarrassing acts which can affect others not in their group – strippers, dares, lewd acts, water fights; and general unpredictability. The thought of being anywhere near these makes me so anxious; just writing about it has given me a headache and feeling of dizziness. I chose not to have a hen party (partly because I have so few close friends), and the only one I have ever attended was exactly like the description here: horrible.

You may wonder why I was in a club in the first place when I met my husband. Why, to dance, of course… For him, it was simply a way to make money and rid himself of aggressive energy as needed. Mostly, he stood in a quiet corner with a glass of lemonade, playing the slot machine and hoping no one would speak to him.

CHAPTER 19

CULTURED HISTORY

The purpose of museums and galleries is to exhibit a multitude of artefacts to stimulate the mind and sometimes the body. There are many ways to do this: visually, audibly, aromatically, through taste, touch or relying on the perception of the mind. For the autistic individual, the possibility of such stimulations can create anticipation of a wonderful experience; for the same reasons, on a different day or time, or depending on circumstances or mood, visiting a museum or gallery can be the most overwhelming and uncomfortable experience.

Many a first impression and memory of being in a museum is as a child, perhaps on a school visit. I remember two museum trips as a child. My first memory of visiting a museum, the British Museum, was during a hospital stay when I was ten; the hospital school teacher took me to Westminster Abbey and the British Museum. I don't remember much, except for the enormity of everything, from the entrance hallway, to the exhibits, to the vast marble columns…as well as my favourite mint choc chip ice cream which she bought me on the way back to the hospital. My second memory was a trip to the Natural History Museum in London, during my secondary (high) school years.

I have visited many museums and galleries over my adult years in many cities; some experiences have been quite disappointing, but so many have been exhilarating and often very tiring as well, mentally and physically, and even at times emotionally. Art, for example, can stir our souls, and often it recalls memories, good and bad.

The exteriors of museums are generally enormous, imposing buildings at first glance, although, of course, there will be exceptions. Many are ornate and feature stonework executed hundreds or thousands of years ago. The first thing I notice as an autistic individual is the space – most have huge hallways, surrounded by beautiful materials such as marble, slate and stone. I often walk around just touching everything – stroking my hands up and down the cool, smooth, hard marble and over the uneven texture of natural slate. I am very tactile, as are many autistic individuals, and I enjoy touching objects to get a sense of their reality and to help me focus. For example, I keep a smooth pebble in the pocket of each of my coats to calm me, and I have a marble pebble on my desk to hold; it helps my focus and concentration when I write. I admit I also put my tongue on it from time to time; the sensation is strangely cooling, and I get hot easily and quickly. This, I am sure, sounds very odd to the non-autistic reader, but it prevents me from overheating and potentially moving towards meltdown.

I love to listen to the plethora of languages being spoken around me in museums and galleries. Does anyone ever really hear other languages, or simply write them off as different and therefore not worth taking any notice of? I find some languages – Chinese for one – intriguing to listen to; sounds more than words seem to be expressed.

Entering the main exhibition rooms of one museum, I observed large white arches, ornate but simple and elegant; rooms were streaming with teenagers probably on a school outing, looking for random objects which were shown or listed on their worksheets. Among the students rushing around was the occasional one who stood poised in front of an exhibition stand, pen in hand, with a look of wonder. I always think that within every exhibition is something that will stop an individual in his or her tracks to just stare. Something just touches your senses and you can't help yourself.

A fascinating exhibition of 19th- and 20th-century clothing in London shows how ornate ladies' fashions once were. The structure of the clothes alone is an absolute work of art. Textures, colours and fabrics, all beautiful; if they were not behind glass, I would want to reach out and touch them. In fact, I find this frustrating; at the risk of being repetitive, I love textures and find myself touching items to get a true vision of their qualities. I think touch is definitely underrated in the non-autistic world. I also find it interesting that clothing of earlier times was mainly of colour, with black only featuring as decoration. I find black to be visually unappealing, and would go as far as saying it can actually hurt my eyes at times when I am feeling particularly overloaded or anxious. There is only one event where I wear black and thankfully that is not very often.

In one large area of this museum, the Victoria and Albert, there is a really wide walkway with entrances into other areas of interest; it is filled with oversized sculptures, each of which would have taken many hundreds if not thousands of hours to create... Yet I noticed on one visit that no one was looking at them; it was as if they were there simply to decorate the room. I am not sure that's what each sculptor had in mind as he or she spent hours on them. It is rather sad that they are not appreciated as they should be. As I touched them, it was as if I felt them in the way the sculptors before me did, drawing inspiration from their own senses.

Within these busy buildings, it is important for me to find quieter 'escape' areas, just for a few minutes, which allow me to be calm and peaceful, and to recharge ready for the next phases of the visit. There are often quiet and quirky corners to be discovered which allow the mind to focus and even to meditate or practise visualisation as necessary.

Despite the potential for fantastic sensory experiences, museums can be bittersweet, lending themselves to potential disappointment – mainly because of other people. One museum I visit is visually perfect for the autistic sensory system: low lighting, muted wall colours and mood lighting giving a satisfying blue glow; my eyes remain comfortable and my head calm.

The main centrepiece of the front entrance is a huge escalator which travels upwards into 'earth'; a ginormous spherical object with the markings of earth and coloured orange-gold. Beyond 'earth' are volcanoes and earthquakes – irresistible with a 'wow' factor. As I enter 'earth', the light, the reflections, the textures, the colours shine out; it is a simply incredible experience which makes me want to go back down and travel up again immediately. The pull of wanting to touch objects here is just irresistible; the textures just beg to be stroked. I need to visually absorb everything and it can be a little overwhelming as there is so much to take in.

On one visit here, though, I didn't bank on the floods of children at the top, blocking my ability to take in all that I see, all that feeds the senses; the children (all visiting on school trips) were EVERYWHERE: close to the exhibitions, sitting on all the seats, sitting in the aisles and on the floor. EVERYWHERE.

It was spectacular as always, but the hordes of children spoilt the sensory experiences. I didn't mind the children per se, but the noise they made was objectionable. I

vowed then to find out when the museum was at its
quietest and visit only during those times. The chaos
made me feel exceedingly hot, as if I could not breathe
properly. I became so flustered that I just wanted to strike
out at anyone who was near to me. I struggled to keep
my composure.

Among the chaos was a beacon of hope as I watched a
young child engaging with one of the hands-on exhibits
in awe, and another young boy was gingerly handling
an exhibit which revealed secrets of the sea; he seemed
absolutely entranced by it. These scenes gave me some
calming moments, where I felt a glimmer of control...
but not enough. I became extremely stressed, and my
body fought to give up walking and just collapse beneath
me. I needed a quiet getaway from it all; I was becoming
grouchy and tired and resenting everything around me.
I recognised some of the early signs that I was going
into sensory overload and I sought a quiet place with
urgency. I could easily have hit out if provoked, but I
never do; I always manage to find a coping strategy
dependent on where I am at the time. Not all autistic
individuals manage to do this, and hitting out, cursing or
shouting is common in some.

I finally found an area where a haunting voice
explained the solar system, and with this exception it
was noise-free. The sensory experience I was expecting
from this museum finally washed over me, comforting
me, soothing me. Suddenly, it was all right again and I
sat there for what seemed like an eternity. In fact, I could
have slept there, it was so relaxing.

I am not normally drawn to science-related culture, but I thought I would leave my comfort zone for a while and give a science museum a try. It was magnificent – quite dark and less formal and stuffy than I imagined; all the exhibits were large and very visual, seemingly placed to be touched. Looking around in wonder, I saw there were life-sized astronauts 'walking on the moon'. I found myself getting so excited that I became very hot and panicked; I managed to bump into one of the exhibits as my sense of direction failed me. In anxiety-ridden situations, my coordination and balance become very dysfunctional. Staying calm is the obvious state to be in, but it is not always easy; this particular time it was the heat and excitement that caused the anxiety, although this may seem strange to you. As usual, I found a 'quiet' place; on this occasion it was in the middle of the floor, leaning against a pillar! As I sat and wrote, no one seemed to take any notice of me; I did not even feel out of place. Hmmm, perhaps they thought I was an exhibit? The loud noises caused by people found at the other museum were still present here, but not as noticeable because the space was bigger, and floors were carpeted rather than laid with stone or marble. This caused less audible sensory disturbance, as sound was muffled.

I was fascinated by the stack of classic cars, and a jet plane hanging from the sky: how cool. I started to feel like a child again – staring in awe at the amazing exhibits. A sudden loud noise made me jump and scream; I was not the only one to wonder about it. Here, children and adults together were utterly engaged in the nearby steam engine with its coughs, splutters and screeches.

Another area of this museum made my senses sing and dance – at times literally. I found the Pattern Pod, and I did not want to leave it. This Pod is really aimed at children, although it doesn't specifically say as much; as an autistic adult, I absolutely fell in love with this area. Everything was designed to appease the senses – every single one of them. There were amazing sounds, countless colours, inviting textures, things to press and pull; I wanted to try them all. Everything was so alluring, so 'touchy-feely', shiny, hard, soft, fluffy, squidgy...

Two areas were particularly satisfying. The first was a large area on the floor which, to the naked eye, had pebbles and fish drawn on it. As people walked over, it swished like the ocean, the image moving with little fish that appeared to be swimming around. This appeals to the autistic individual who is sensitive to visual and audio textures. It is also very tactile in that it made me want to run my hands over it to 'feel' the water swishing, even though my mind really knew it was just a smooth floor. The children were intently trying to catch the fish as they appeared to move about. Others simply crossed it with funny walks, creeping, running and so on, trying to get it to move to their beat. They were just as captivated by it as I was. As a calming strategy, I have an app on my smartphone which enables images to be overlaid with rippling water as the screen is touched; this is a similar effect and useful for autistic individuals.

The second area was the dancing room. Just the name filled me with hope, but it was far simpler than I imagined. There was a wall which showed images of the museum visitors dancing or standing and waving their arms in front of it, with different effects. As the dancing and the music changed, the effects and patterns changed. It is quite difficult to describe, but it was tremendous fun – a bit like the mirror room in the fairground where the images change when you move about, depending on which mirror you stand in front of. For the autistic individual who finds physical body positioning fascinating, this would be a positive experience. I know of autists who frequently pose in front of a mirror to get a firm perspective of who they really are.

Many autistic individuals can be childlike in their passions and their perspectives and reactions to the world. We see fun in things and have a very literal sense of what goes on. We can also be brutally honest about what we see and hear. These traits are all akin to children. An autistic adult friend, sadly no longer with us, had an incredible passion for adventures and games, many of which would have seemed dangerous to you and me. They lit him up, his face awash with excitement. He loved to climb trees, fly in small planes, experiment with all kinds of activities with an acute intensity, and then would quickly lose interest in them, just like a child.

This type of museum could have been very overwhelming, but the low lighting and feeling of space throughout prevented this. I would definitely recommend a visit if you find yourself in a city with a science museum.

As an autistic individual, I notice details – not just the obvious details, but the very smallest ones which have been painstakingly created by an artist, an architect, a carpenter or a stonemason. These kinds of details are ever-present in many museums, galleries and monuments worldwide – the Taj Mahal, for example, a monument I admire in pictures but have yet to see in person.

A favourite art gallery is one where exquisite detail is in abundance; each room has a high ceiling, incredibly ornate with precise curvatures and mouldings; the lighting is a dream for most autistic individuals, with natural light streaming in from the ceiling, and the spotlights are all off, presumably used only for darker days and evenings. The natural lighting gives the feeling of being outside while actually being inside, an art 'conservatory' of sorts. Every wing of the building has its own opulent jewel-like colour; bold and rich sumptuous fabrics such as brocades cover the walls, where they form a stunning backdrop for the highlights of the gallery: the artwork. Paintings here are varied – some dark and, in my opinion, quite eerie, others calm and peaceful. I love to just wander through the rooms, stopping to admire, question or simply observe the plethora of work from hugely talented individuals.

When I close my eyes for a brief moment, there is no discernible aroma – perhaps just the faint smell of musk. After all, many of the *objets d'art* are centuries old; gone is the smell of oil paint, but as they mature another aroma replaces the original.

Because the light is not artificial, it is calming for the eyes and a welcome rest from the assault on my senses from the rest of a city visit. Despite the crowds of people, it feels peaceful, even in the middle of a capital city which can be utterly exhausting if you try to take in too much at once.

I love to hear the sound of footsteps across the wooden floors as people wander, watch and analyse. What are they thinking? Older children are discussing the paintings, which makes me smile, and then suddenly I hear 'Let's go to the gift shop'. Considering the children in the gallery, I wonder if true appreciation comes as we get older, or only as we are inspired, and is not affected by age at all.

My favourite paintings are those surrounded by water – the canals and bridges of Venice in particular. Strangely, I have sensory deficits when it comes to water, as I have explained in previous chapters, and my biggest dark fear is death by drowning. I have, however, always found myself drawn to the sea, canals, rivers; watching water slowly rippling is very calming, I find. In art, I equally love paintings which incorporate these images; the city of Venice with its never-ending waterways running through the city and the romance of the gondola cruising around the lagoon in real life is exactly how the 'Venice Room' shows itself to me. I lose myself in the art and I am back in Venice; that is exactly what art should do.

Many people tour this gallery with an audio guide through headphones, but although this gives order to the tour, I fear they have closed off their senses. Or is it their way to focus on the central importance here: the art itself. I don't believe this gallery is simply about the art but about the building, the ambience and the people. After all, there would be none of these things without people being inspired in some way.

'They are the books, the arts, the academies, that show, contain, and nourish the world.'

William Shakespeare (Love's Labour's Lost)

There is no doubt that many people visit cities for the cultural experiences. Although I feel at ease in this area, I recognise that there are other ways to entertain myself, and so I push on to try things I would not necessarily choose in a 'pick and mix' of options.

CHAPTER 20

LIVING A THEME

Autistic individuals with hypo-reactive vestibular systems – that is, they continually need to stimulate with sounds and motion – actively seek intense sensory experiences. This is perhaps where themed attractions are ideal. Personally, they are not generally my favourite type of entertainment as I never know what to expect or how engaged I need to be, but I like to give new experiences a chance, and I have been known to enjoy some entertainment, loosely labelled within this themed area.

I have loved shows at the London and New York Planetariums. They provide astronomy-themed shows, often combined with music of varying types. One show combined the music of Jean-Michel Jarre (a French composer, specialising in electronic and ambient music) with spectacular lasers and lights. Sitting on the floor of the planetarium watching the laser show above me to his incredible music was an experience I have never forgotten. For some autists, it may be too much sensory stimulation, but I have always loved fireworks, especially to music, so for me this was magnificent – quite simply electric. I could feel the music running through my veins, and seeing the lasers at the same time only enhanced the feelings, sending shivers down my body. Another show was to Mike Oldfield's *Tubular Bells*. Again, incredible music; for me, it has so much texture and depth. It is my musical equivalent of stroking velvet and popping bubble wrap.

The Empire State Building in New York is an attraction, not so much themed, but one which tourists around the world visit; it is one of the tallest in the city, reaching 102 floors. At night the building changes colour according to various events and in recognition of partner organisations and causes. In April, for example, the building turns blue for autism, along with hundreds of other buildings around the world. How incredible that autism is celebrated in this way!

The building features exhibitions, restaurants and the most stunning marble art deco-style lobby; the ceiling features elegant murals, and even the escalators are elegant. Everywhere there is something spectacular to look at or to touch, which is a severely underrated sense for non-autistic people. If it looks inviting, why would you not touch it? Of course, for most, going up to the very top and looking at the spectacular views over the city is the most popular reason for a visit; for me, it was following in the footsteps of Cary Grant in one of my favourite movies, *An Affair to Remember*, where he was to meet with Deborah Kerr. I hate heights, the lifts were jam-packed with people, queues waited to go up and down to each level, but it was worth the effort and the excruciating discomfort as I stood in his shadow; the views were absolutely amazing. There is plenty to stimulate the senses here, but if you dislike crowds or being bumped into, perhaps you should consider quieter times of the day; it is open until 2am, so there is plenty of choice.

A completely new experience for me was to visit the site of the original home belonging to Sherlock Holmes which had been made into a museum of sorts to pay tribute to the eccentric sleuth, ironically purported to have been autistic. The front door, opened by a policeman, led up narrow passages and stairs into Sherlock Holmes' rooms. Although it was cozy, with dark period colours and burning log fires, it was also quite stifling for me. Each room was small and filled with artefacts of the man himself: pipes, detecting equipment, pistols and his famous deerstalker hat. There was a kind of eeriness, but at the same time it was welcoming, with many mannequins and busts about the place. It also had a musty smell, which oddly I enjoyed; it smelled of past lives and times, somehow allowing me to be transported back to another period. Other visitors took turns in wearing the deerstalker and posing for photos, but I chose not to do this. The thought of wearing a hat worn by many hundreds of others filled me with horror and anxiety. It is akin to wearing shoes at a bowling alley worn by others – completely abhorrent. I did like the ability to touch the artefacts and really get a feel for them, rather than them being behind glass as in larger museums. Sadly, I didn't spend long here as the crowds of visitors made the small spaces hot and uncomfortable, and I soon had a headache and needed air quickly before panic set in.

Now, for the next experience you need a good imagination, but if you don't possess one, I shall try to describe the detail to you. In Orlando, Florida, Joe and I decided (on my part reluctantly) to visit a ghostly attraction. Again, it was not really my thing, but he loves anything connected with ghosts or ghouls. We joined six other people at the start of the tour and were instructed to stand in a line and hold on to each other's shoulders as we walked around. Joe, being the tallest, stood at the back with me in front of him. In front of me was a young man who wore his jeans hanging down loosely. I just knew this was going to be a disaster; I didn't really want to touch him and was already anxious.

As we walked around, spooks and ghostly figures came out of nowhere to scare us; things fell down from the ceiling on top of us; odours, screams, blood...you get the picture. I was hating every moment of the experience; even Joe seemed to be spooked, but he was trying to laugh it all off. The others in the group spent most of the time screaming, and by this time most of our hands had moved down to the waist to keep hold as people continued to get frightened and were jumping about. Towards the end of the tour, we had to walk across the rickety rope bridge, when suddenly a large scary-looking (understatement) man dressed all in black, with blood all over his face, put a hand on Joe's back. Joe spun round, screamed loudly and pushed forward in panic, causing the whole line of people to fall on to our fronts. Suddenly, the place lit up, and as we looked up, we found that Joe had pushed us through the door into the gift shop, which was filled with people staring at us all lying on the floor, face down. We were totally mortified, of course, but suddenly we all started to laugh. Joe and I must have spent ten minutes or so on the floor hysterically laughing, before someone eventually helped us up. The other fallen visitors had already gone by then, embarrassed by the event, especially the young man in front of me as his trousers were pulled down as we collapsed in a heap. Autistic individuals can often laugh uncontrollably or cry inappropriately – laughing at a funeral, for example.

I have never let Joe forget the evening, and to this day it is a story to retell at social occasions where we don't know what else to say. It makes people laugh and we no longer feel uncomfortable. Perhaps that is the key to social functions for us autists: have a few choice stories ready to tell if necessary. Better to be laughed *with* than laughed *at*.

I shall end this chapter with one of my favourite places in New York: Radio City.

The auditorium is 160 feet from the back to the stage and the ceiling is 84 feet high. It boasts sweeping arches and a beautiful golden stage curtain. The whole building is very art deco in style and has incredible architecture and ornate decoration throughout. Most exciting for me is the ambience and the history of the great stars who have appeared on the grand stage. Favourites of mine, Cary Grant, Sammy Davis Jnr and Frank Sinatra, have all appeared on the stage and I walked on it myself. It made me feel like doing a little tap dance so that I could say I had danced on the same stage as Sammy Davis Jnr, or for that matter a Rockette (the glamorous in-house dancers). Everywhere in Radio City pacified my senses – the beautiful sights, the unnerving silence with such history enveloping the air, the glamour – and I spent most of the tour touching and feeling the luxurious fabrics, the marble and the gilt decoration. It was simply stunning.

More than that, though, was the annual Christmas show held here; I had the pleasure of experiencing this just recently for the first time. It began a little scary with the considerable depth of the crowds outside and around the few blocks surrounding the venue. Once inside, we just stood together in hordes around each of the entrances to the auditorium. Joe started to get panicky, but we concentrated on going in, and within seconds of the doors opening, the crowds had dissipated; never have I seen such organisation and efficient staff at an event so big.

There was amazing space between seats, and everything felt so relaxed. We were entertained before the show by two massive vintage multilayered organs, which came out from the curtains and then retreated as the show began. The orchestra emerged out of the floor at one point, and then receded again. We were given 3D glasses to watch Santa 'fly around' New York City, delivering gifts, landing at Radio City to host the show. The symmetry of the dancers, the colours, the large-scale scenery, and the sounds…the show was the most amazing I had ever seen. If you want your senses to be tickled – to be assaulted really, but in the best way possible – I urge you to visit when you can.

I hope I get to return one day. There really is nothing like it…that I have seen so far!

CHAPTER 21

THRILL OF THE CROWD

Street entertainers are usually more than people trying to make some extra cash. Often they are professionals who perform in the streets to gain recognition, practise new skills or routines, or simply perform in the streets for a living. Songwriter and singer Paul Simon and his former partner Art Garfunkel started music careers by busking in the streets of London and other European cities. The late great Robin Williams earned his way through Juilliard School with a mime act outside the Museum of Modern Art. Even legendary blues and jazz performer B.B. King began as a young boy playing his guitar on the streets of Mississippi.

I have seen some great street entertainers, but I am also very wary of them in case they try to call up members of the audience and I get embarrassed. They seem to have an eye for those who are trying to avoid engaging, and single them out. It is the unexpected I shy away from; I simply don't know what they expect of me, and finding out in front of an amused audience who are grateful it's not them is not my idea of fun. My panic appears to make me stand out and I can just see them looking at me, getting ready to pounce. Of course, that is probably just my perception and not reality at all. Autistic individuals tend not to like the unexpected and would avoid these situations if possible.

In the Introduction, I wrote about the silver man who was balancing, and I have seen several similar acts in a variety of cities. There have also been jugglers, fire eaters, singers, musicians, comedians, mime artists, those who ride unicycles, magicians…and the list goes on. I love that they just perform wherever they are, but for autistic individuals, they might not always be a positive experience. If I am just walking around a city trying to work out directions, or I am feeling quite overloaded, bumping into a street entertainer making loud noises or having jeering crowds in my way might be what tips me over the edge.

On a visit to Covent Garden, famous in London for its street entertainers, I came across a man sitting on a street corner playing (blowing through) a traffic cone. He was clearly not a professional and was not trying to attract a crowd as the others do in this area. He was just playing the theme from *The Flintstones* over and over again with hat in front of him. I went into a shop, looked around for ten minutes or so, and when I came out he was still playing the same tune. He was brave enough to take advantage of an everyday object and just have a go. How I admired him. I happen to love *The Flintstones*; I was humming it all day! He made me smile and that's what entertainment is all about. How I would love the confidence to dance in the street as if no one was watching!

Street entertainers can be loud, and this can cause me pain sometimes, especially if there is sudden noise, but the most difficult sensation for me is the feeling of the audience all around me – like being trapped in a crowded lift with no way of escaping. If I am in the middle of a crowd and try to get out, I either bump into people in my panic to get away or find myself constantly excusing myself as I weave out of the crowd, which can attract the attention of the performer.

While I try to avoid being at the front or in the middle of the crowd watching street entertainers, I do love to watch from the back. I have heard some fantastic music, watched some amazing stunt tricks, and heard some great singing. I have also come across terrible but brave street entertainers. Just the other day, I was walking past a department store in a city centre; a woman was sitting on the ground, banging a tambourine while singing. It was actually hurting my ears. According to the city cleaner who was emptying bins, she had been there every day for a week. Although her entertainment was not to my taste and caused me excruciating pain, as I watched around me, everyone noticed her; some even gave her money.

I was quite impressed by the woman's gutsy determination to do what she loved, or perhaps what she thought she was good at. She didn't give up or care if people judged her. Perhaps a lesson for us all?

CONCLUSION

Well, we finally reach the end of my sensory journey. I hope you have gained something from reading about it.

Cities are, at their very best, enormous galleries filled with myriad buildings, people and sensory 'candy', which can be tasty but not always the best thing for you. Although I may feel comfortable with a particular experience, another person might feel overwhelmed and disconcerted. Each individual's perspective of the city is subjective and unique, and will have its highs and lows. This perspective, for an autistic individual, can be dependent on many variables including the time of day or year, mood, levels of anxiety... Often, we have a tendency to opt for the familiar: hotels regularly used, shops and parts of cities we know better than others, restaurants or coffee shops we enjoy.

I have tried more recently to experience living in the city in a different way: by leaving my comfort zone in search of new and, I hope, exciting experiences. This has not always been easy, but as an autistic individual I try to find ways to handle difficult situations, rather than avoid them completely. Despite common autism theory that we are not creative, I would have to disagree to some extent as I think we are forced to be creative in many environments so that we can manage the uncomfortable and often painful situations we find ourselves in. I try to meditate internally, I use a silent mantra, I close my eyes and just breathe, I even write a shopping list in my head or plan the week's dinner menu – all ways to 'drown out' any difficulties around me. If all else fails, I try to find something or someone who makes me smile to focus on. This may be a lovely hat, a small child laughing, a poster with an interesting photo or even simply the buildings around me.

A young child is generally happy to respond to anyone around him without restrictions or expectations placed on him by society. There is no habit formed to prevent him from interacting or engaging with experiences. Autistic individuals can often be childlike: in the literal thinking and speaking, the excitement of a passion, the disappointment or 'tantrum' when things don't go their way, the constant questions... How wonderful to be forever young.

Take a chance, visit the city of your dreams, and enjoy the experience. Remember to have backup strategies, though – just in case!

REFERENCES

An Affair to Remember (1957) Directed by Leo McCarey [Film]. USA: 20th Century Fox.

Beale-Ellis, S.J. (2015) *Autism and Martial Arts: A Guide for Children, Parents and Teachers.* Kent: NAKMAS Publishing.

Bogdashina, O. (2016) *Sensory Perceptual Issues in Autism and Asperger Syndrome*, 2nd Edition. London: Jessica Kingsley Publishers.

Cheers (1982–1993) Produced by Charles/Barrows/Charles Productions [Television]. USA: Paramount Network Television.

Dahl, R. (1972) *Charlie and the Great Glass Elevator.* New York, NY: Alfred A. Knopf.

Ellis, C. (2004) *The Ethnographic I: A Methodological Novel about Autoethnography.* Walnut Creek, CA: AltaMira Press.

Frith, U. (2003) *Autism: Explaining the Enigma.* Oxford: Blackwell Publishing.

Haddon, M. (2004) *The Curious Incident of the Dog in the Night-Time.* London: Vintage.

Lawson, W. (2011) *The Passionate Mind: How People with Autism Learn.* London: Jessica Kingsley Publishers.

Lee, H. (1960) *To Kill a Mockingbird.* London: Pan Books.

Up in the Air (2009) Directed by Jason Reitman [Film]. USA: Paramount Pictures.

A FEW RESOURCES

WEBSITES

www.theautisticvoice.co.uk My professional website, including a link to my blog, The Autistic Voice.

www.nas.org.uk The National Autistic Society is a charity that supports all aspects of autism in the United Kingdom. The website includes lots of information about training, events, advocacy and research.

www.autism-society.org The Autism Society is the USA's leading grassroots autism organisation. It works to increase public awareness about the day-to-day issues affecting people across the spectrum, advocate for appropriate services for individuals of every age, and provide the latest information regarding treatment, education, research and advocacy.

www.bwy.org.uk The British Wheel of Yoga: to find classes in your area. I recommend you try a few classes to find the right teacher for you.

www.yogaalliance.org The Yoga Alliance is based in the USA. It is a good starting point to find a qualified yoga teacher in your area.

MOBILE PHONE APPLICATIONS

Mindfulness: The Art of Being Human (Reuben Lowe) This is fantastic for starting a meditation practice.

Relax Lite: Stress and Anxiety Relief (Saagara) I use this for both meditation and breathing practice; it helps me to get to sleep on flights.

Beale-Ellis, Sandra.

MANTRA

Sensing the city.

A mantra is a phrase you say over and over to yourself to calm anxieties, when you have a need to slow your breathing or just to relax. For example, 'I am becoming calm and quiet' or 'I can get through this by breathing'. The phrase can be whatever you wish to feel at that moment.